T0105624

Jim Leuschen's book *The Lost Gospel of the First Christians* is a brilliant challenge to the modern Church to restore the Gospel that was preached in the early days following Christ's resurrection. Calling us to recognize the center of the apostles' preaching as the resurrection, rather than Christ's death on the cross, Jim recaptures the New Testament's focus on Christ's victory over death as the essence of His triumph. While never failing to honor the importance of Christ's death, he demonstrates the centrality and power of the resurrection in a most convincing way. In a simple, systematic way, Jim builds, layer upon layer, the foundational truths of the basic gospel. He lines up each *domino* in such a way that much clarity is brought to our understanding. This book would make a great course for new believers. For many older believers it would challenge many unbiblical ideas that have been taught and embraced by many in the Church for many years. I highly recommend this book!

Joe McIntyre
Founder and Senior Minister
Word of His Grace Church
President, Kenyon's Gospel Publishing Society

Doctrinal tenets considered most basic to the faith should be directly traceable to those things which the earliest apostles believed and taught. If the original apostles didn't teach something, and yet, we emphasize it today, this should be a flag for us. It certainly should be a matter for closer examination and dialogue. What Jim has accomplished through this book is something unprecedented. By carefully guiding us through the earliest development of doctrine and practice, he prompts his readers to question, in a healthy way, a number of things that we all might have otherwise taken for granted as foundational. May we have the courage to *go there* with Jim, and then, to further weigh the implications of this ground-breaking work. This truly is a bombshell!

Daryl Wood
Author and prophetic teacher

This is a well written and carefully crafted study and work that speaks to us today from a very Hebrew perspective. It allows the reader to see and hear the gospel of the Kingdom in the way that early believers did, through the death, burial and resurrection of Yahshua. Jim has done a masterful job in bringing to light a very different view that is destined to challenge your present understanding. It is an honor and a privilege to recommend this book to you and it is my hope that it will be widely distributed and read by all and I pray that it becomes a written reference that you will cherish for life.

Blake L. Higginbotham
Cyrus Apostolic Ministries & Professions

The Lost Gospel of the First Christians

The Original First-Generation Foundation
You've Been Missing

James E. Leuschen

WESTBOW
PRESS
A DIVISION OF THOMAS NELSON

WestBow Press books may be ordered through booksellers or by contacting:

WestBow Press
A Division of Thomas Nelson
1663 Liberty Drive
Bloomington, IN 47403
www.westbowpress.com
1-(866) 928-1240

Because of the dynamic nature of the Internet, any web addresses or links contained in this book may have changed since publication and may no longer be valid. The views expressed in this work are solely those of the author and do not necessarily reflect the views of the publisher, and the publisher hereby disclaims any responsibility for them.

Any people depicted in stock imagery provided by Thinkstock are models, and such images are being used for illustrative purposes only. Certain stock imagery © Thinkstock.

Scripture quotations are taken from the New King James Version, Copyright 1982 by Thomas Nelson, Inc. Used by permission. All rights reserved.
Front Cover Image: Raphael Sanzio (1483-1520), Study for St. Paul Preaching in Athens, Galleria degli Uffizi, Florence, Italy
Back Cover Image: Raphael (Raffaello Sanzio) (1483-1520), Eight Apostles, c. 1514. Woodner Collection, 1993.51.2, Image courtesy of the National Gallery of Art, Washington, D.C.

ISBN: 978-1-4497-7552-0 (e)
ISBN: 978-1-4497-7553-7 (sc)
ISBN: 978-1-4497-7554-4 (hc)

Library of Congress Control Number: 2012921406
Printed in the United States of America

WestBow Press rev. date: 1/30/2013

Contents

[In the earliest days of Christianity] to preach Christianity meant primarily to preach the Resurrection... The resurrection is the central theme in every Christian sermon reported in the Acts. The Resurrection, and its consequences, were the "gospel" or good news which the Christians brought: what we call the "gospels," the narratives of our Lord's life and death, were composed later for the benefit of those who had already accepted the gospel. They were in no sense the basis of Christianity: they were written for those already converted. The miracle of the Resurrection, and the theology of that miracle, comes first: the biography comes later as a comment on it.

The New Testament writers speak as if Christ's achievement in rising from the dead was the first event of its kind in the whole history of the universe. He is the "first fruits," the "pioneer of life." He has forced open a door that has been locked since the death of the first man. He has met, fought, and beaten the King of Death. Everything is different because He has done so. This is the beginning of the New Creation: a new chapter in cosmic history has been opened.

C.S. Lewis

Introduction

The gospel—in its original, pristine form!

The contents of this book may surprise you. By reading it you allow me to lead you on a journey of discovery. I hope to open your eyes to something amazing—the original structure of the gospel for the first generation of Christians.[1] May you witness to its newborn simplicity and power, just as it unfolded in the first thirty to forty years of its proclamation. May you grasp it like those Hebrew-oriented first believers did—without any later developments.

Of course, what the church came to believe after the first century merits close attention and scrutiny. Later church controversies profoundly shaped gospel proclamation and teaching. Some of those controversies lasted hundreds of years. Students of church history can appreciate the ongoing contributions to Christian doctrine and practice made by the saints through the ages.

Those later contributions, however, are not of concern here. Let no one be misled as to my intentions here in writing this volume. As you read it you will not find the claim that all doctrinal developments after the first generation were mistaken. Neither is my purpose in writing to inform you perfectly on every key Christian doctrine. No, this writing has one single-minded

---

1   No concept presented here relies on second-generation material. In a few cases, footnotes will quote also from second-generation sources—particularly the writings of John—but never alone, without first-generation documentation.

objective: to take you into the first century to grasp the teaching of the full gospel message preached by Peter, Paul, and the other disciples of the Lord Jesus, mostly prior to the destruction of Jerusalem in AD 70.[2] Doctrine emerging after that time is not in view.

The complete message preached by the early church was somewhat like a series of interlocking propositions. That is how I have chosen to break down the message. These propositions naturally tend to build from one statement to the next, leading to a climax. I list the complete set of points at the end of the book, but I develop these propositions from the beginning of the book two at a time, indicating them as though they were "dominoes." (The first domino knocks over the second, the second knocks over the third, and so on.) These propositions bring structure, order, simplicity and coherence to the gospel message preached by the apostles of the first century.

From the start, the reader needs to be aware of two caveats. First, as I set forth the gospel of the first generation of Christians, I am not proving a historically verifiable reconstruction of exactly how things developed. That is a task no one can do because there isn't enough actual historical information available. But historians do have sufficient data to put enough pieces together to set forth some general observations with confidence.

Second, some of the propositions in the chapters below may have been expounded by Paul or his disciples, but not in the same way or to the same degree by Peter or the other apostles. That is okay, since this observation does not contradict the thesis of this book. The book of Acts[3] makes it clear that although Peter and Paul—two very different people—preached to different target

2   Either Paul's death or the fall of Jerusalem could serve equally well here. The date for a dividing line between the first and second generation of Christians is an interesting issue, but the thesis of this book does not actually depend on any historical data external to the contents of Scripture.

3   See also Gal 1:18–24.

audiences[4] with different issues, the two had basically the same foundation. I bring you that foundation in this small book—a foundation of truth to last for eternity.

4   Gal 2:7.

Orientation

The faith that Jesus and his apostles delivered once for all[5] was "for the Jew first, and also for the Greek."[6] Whatever else that means, it certainly means that the good news, properly understood in our day, should be intelligible and meaningful to a first-century Jew. The point here is that, in some ways, the gospel that went forth in the first century doesn't look quite like what Christians often teach today. Today's believers need to discover how it looked back then and to recover foundations.

To begin with, the early disciples knew their truth claims of the good news, the kingdom of God, and Jesus had to be substantiated by the Old Testament Scriptures.[7] To them, they were not originating a brand new way to think about God and his truth which would then be developed over the centuries. Instead, they saw themselves at the end of an era, at the climax of Israel's long history, in the time of the fulfillment of the great promises that God had made to his people.[8] This insight is important. Without it one will never really understand how the gospel actually unfolded.

The original gospel teaching was a seamless revelation from start to finish. Every part related closely to every other part. To become aware of this interrelatedness is crucial for understanding. To

---

5   Jude 3.

6   Ro 1:16. Also Ro 2:9; 3:29–30; 9:24.

7   Ac 26:22–23; 2Ti 3:16–17; Ro 15:4; 1Co 10:11.

8   Heb 1:2; 9:26; Eph 1:10; 1Pe 1:20; 2Pe 3:3; 1Jn 2:18; Jude 18.

change part of one's gospel foundation—any truth, emphasis, or insight—without paying attention to the rest, is to fail to grasp its essential coherence. When Christians pigeonhole certain doctrines without looking carefully at their entire scheme of doctrinal beliefs, they miss those subtle but important connections that tie everything together.

For clarity, let it be said that the set of interlocking propositions below may be linked to one another in more than one way, once I develop the true beginning point: the resurrection of Jesus.

"THE DOMINOES" —
Sixteen Points of Truth

First Point of Truth: The Resurrection of Jesus

A. Jesus of Nazareth, crucified on a cross, has been raised bodily from the dead into glorified, everlasting life.

B. It was God—the God of the Jews—who raised Jesus from the dead, thus declaring Jesus to be God's "special agent" to accomplish his will and purpose.

The gospel begins with an astounding claim, that God raised Jesus from the dead.[9] This is to make the starting point of faith a question of fact and not theory or theology. To say it another way, the gospel stands or falls on the objective reality of Jesus' resurrection.[10]

Faith in a resurrection demands some kind of evidence. The resurrection faith of the earliest believers was founded on real evidence that Jesus had risen from the grave. They had become convinced of the truth for many reasons—not least the empty tomb, the post-resurrection appearances of the Lord to his disciples, and the unfolding revelation that in Jesus' resurrection Old Testament prophecy had been fulfilled.

---

9   Ro 1:1–4; Ac 2:29–40; 5:30–31; 10:38–42; 13:32–35, 36–39. Once the reader's eyes are opened, Scriptures like this become numerous.

10   1Co 15:14–19.

In addition, first-century Jews were on the lookout for the coming of God's new era of fulfillment.[11] For every such Jew, the dynamic activity of the Holy Spirit—as Paul said, "in demonstration of the Spirit and of power"[12]—would have supplied evidence for the gospel's truth. Luke reports that "with great power the apostles gave witness to the resurrection of the Lord Jesus, and great grace was upon them all."[13] "And the hand of the Lord was with them, and a great number believed and turned to the Lord."[14] Through miracles and demonstrations of power, the Spirit of God witnessed to the truth of the resurrection of Jesus. The earliest disciples had plenty of evidence to help them on the way to genuine faith.

What about today? Again, just as in the case of the early church—and all through church history—the gospel stands or falls on the objective reality of Jesus' resurrection. But if this seems obvious, it isn't. Modern theologians often argue that the Easter faith transcends reason and is confirmed not by the facts of history but only by personal intuitive experience. Bible-believing Christians may sing, "You ask me how I know He lives? He lives within my heart." On the contrary, the gospel does not get its foundation from the domain of subjective impressions. Once exposed as deficient, such thinking calls for a fresh investigation of the faith. The true gospel faith is faith not because believers merely assume that Jesus is somehow alive in some subjective, non-historical, non-bodily, spiritual way. The gospel faith is faith because we claim something happened (A, above), and we make a claim concerning what it means (B, above). The gospel is rooted in an event of history, and in the compelling evidence[15] that confirms that event. The event itself demands an interpretation, and in

---

11   Mt 11:3; Lk 2:25; 2:38; 3:15; 23:51; Ac 1:6.

12   1 Co 2:4.

13   Acts 4:33.

14   Acts 11:21.

15   Evidence for the resurrection is an extremely important subject, but beyond the immediate scope of inquiry.

light of Jesus' life and ministry and the confirming activity of the Holy Spirit, only one interpretation makes any sense: God himself raised Jesus from the dead. This means God had chosen Jesus of Nazareth to be his special agent to reveal his will and purpose for humanity.

It will come as a shock to many people to discover that when the Scriptures refer to the core content of the original faith, it is just this first item of truth above to which they unanimously point.[16] *They point not so much to the blood, the atonement or the death of Christ but chiefly to his resurrection.*[17]

In fact, the Scriptures that reveal the content of the faith fall into two categories. First there are those passages that point to God's act of raising Jesus from the dead.[18] Second are those that emphasize Jesus' status as the Son of God.[19] But the second category depends upon the first. Jesus was declared to be the Son of God with power by his resurrection from the dead.[20] The preeminent title *Son of*

---

16   Mk 16:13–17; Lk 24:25–27, 24:40–47; Jn 2:22, 3:18, 36, 6:69, 9:35, 11:25–27, 20:8, 25, 29, 31; Ac 8:37, 10:43–45, 13:28–34, 36–39, 26:22–23, 27; Ro 1:1–5, 4:24, 6:8–9, 10:9–10; 1Co 15:1–4, 11–14, 17; 2Co 4:13–14; Eph 1:19–20; Col 2:12; 1Th 4:14; 1Pe 1:3–5, 20–21; 1 Jn 5:1, 5.

17   One isolated verse seems to some to point to the contrary. However, that objection cannot be sustained because a careful examination of the literal Greek in Ro 3:25 leaves open the object of faith. The New King James Version translates, "…whom God set forth as a propitiation by his blood, through faith, to demonstrate his righteousness …" Actually, the faith here may be Christ's own faithfulness and not the believer's faith at all!

18   Mk 16:13–17; Lk 24:25–27, 40–47; Jn 2:22, 11:25–27; 20:8, 25, 29; Ac 10:40–43; 13:28–34, 36–39; 26:22–23, 27; Ro 1:1–5; 4:24; 10:9–10; 1Co 15:1–4, 11–14, 17; 1Co 4:13–14; Eph 1:19–20; Col 2:12; 1Th 4:14; 1Pe 1:3–5, 20–21.

19   Jn 3:18, 36; 6:69; 9:35; 11:25–27; 20:31; Ac 8:37; Ro 1:1–5, 1; Jn 5:1, 5.

20   Ro 1:1–5; Ps 2:7.

5

God[21] that believers give to Jesus is based squarely upon the fact that God raised him from the dead.[22]

Further examination of this line of thinking reveals the crux of the connection. Jesus' primary identity on Earth, to those who knew him, was that of rabbi. He was the master teacher, interpreting the Torah and the will of God, instructing the disciples and the multitudes in the true way of life—the way he himself followed. And his resurrection means that his character was vindicated. Now in the Jewish understanding, character includes all of one's actions and words. This means, in turn, that everything Jesus said was validated as truth. God proved in Jesus' resurrection that Jesus' instruction—by which he lived—was the true way. He embodied his own words and was resurrected bodily. By his resurrection he proved that his very words had eternal life and that he could and would make good on every one of his promises. He validated his teaching and promises by his own durability. This means, of course, that his words had God-backed authority, identifying him in retrospect as the coming prophet, who would be like Moses, whose words Israel must fully hear.[23]

The resurrection of Jesus was the kind of miracle that could be recognized by his Jewish contemporaries as God's authenticating signature on the life of Jesus.

In addition, the Old Testament had two criteria by which to declare genuine any supposed prophet. The first is that he must teach in the name of the Yahweh and not try to divert people to the worship of other gods.[24] Jesus fulfilled this criterion. He spoke

---

21 The term *son of God* deserves special attention and separate treatment, but to unpack the meaning of this term would take the reader outside the immediate scope of inquiry.

22 Paul was thinking similarly when he wrote that "Christ died and rose and lived again that he might be Lord" (Ro 14:9).

23 Dt 18:15; Ac 3:22-23.

24 Dt 18:20.

in the name of Yahweh, and he affirmed the Shema,[25] the great Hebrew admonition to honor Yahweh alone. He directed the Jews to worship Yahweh, the God of Israel. The second criterion was that if the prophet makes a prophecy about the future, it must come to pass.[26] Mark's gospel tells us Jesus predicted both his passion and resurrection explicitly on three separate occasions.[27]

Furthermore, Jesus' resurrection validated his identity in at least three significant ways. First he said he would lay down his own life for sins.[28] But God must receive any such sacrifice or else it is invalid. Jesus, in effect, predicted that God would receive the sacrifice. The resurrection, again, is the key. It shows that God approved of the sacrifice and must therefore have received it. Second, Jesus' resurrection partially fulfilled his prediction that all humans would be raised from the dead.[29] Once raised, Jesus demonstrated that resurrection was not only possible, it could happen to human beings in general. And third, Jesus in his humanity was lifted to a new level of existence in his resurrection. During his ministry, Jesus had claimed a special divine status for himself. In coming to life again as he did, Jesus showed that he had supernatural status; that is, that he really was the Son of God. After his resurrection Jesus himself explained to his disciples how both his suffering and his entering into glory were predicted by the prophets in the Old Testament.[30]

For all of these reasons and more, Jesus' resurrection revealed him to be that prophet, like Moses, whom Israel must hear,[31] and

25   Mk 12:29–30; Dt 6:4, 5.

26   Dt 18:21–22.

27   Mk 8:31; 9:31; 10:33–34.

28   Mt 26:26–28; Mk 14:2–24; Lk 22:19–20.

29   Jn 5:28–29.

30   Lk 24:25–26, 44–46; Jn 1:21.

31   Dt 18:15; Ac 3:22-23.

declared him to be the Son of God "with power."[32] Over and over again the New Testament sets forth Jesus' identity as the crucial content of biblical faith. That content was determined not by the cross standing alone but especially through the resurrection.

The next point of truth expands on this first point and unveils its startling implications.

---

32   Ro 1:4.

Second Point of Truth: The Crucified Messiah

A. Jesus is the Anointed One, the Jewish Messiah, the Christ predicted by the Torah and all the prophets.

B. The Jews—in effect—crucified their own Messiah!

First-century Jews witnessed supposed wonder workers before and after Jesus, and his miracles alone could not prove to them that he was their Messiah.[33] Certainly his teaching, though different, could not establish this claim. What about his death on the cross for sins? Many Jews, innocent and guilty, had died on crosses. In the minds of the Jews there was nothing special about that; they did not associate death on a cross with the redemption of sin. What, then, established Jesus as the one promised to come and save Israel? *The first point of truth (domino) establishes the second point of truth (domino). Everything hinged on the resurrection of Jesus from the dead.*

History discloses that first-century Jews expected their Messiah at any time.[34] Judaism could barely accept that the Messiah would suffer and die. What they could not stomach was the idea

---

33   Dt 13:1-3.

34   Mt 11:3; Lk 2:25; 2:38; 3:15; 23:51; Jn 1:19–25; Ac 1:6.

that he would die by crucifixion[35]—as one cursed by the law and condemned by its guardians. At issue was not the idea of resurrection itself but whether God would resurrect this particular man, vindicating a crucified apostate who had been executed for undermining the Torah. So Judaism's denial of Jesus' resurrection rested not on historical evidence but on theological grounds. To them, if Jesus' resurrection contradicted the Holy Scriptures, then that settled the issue—it could not have happened.[36] At stake was the authority of the Torah, the law of Moses.

Consider how this works. The law code in Deuteronomy specifically backed the decisions of the Torah's guardians.[37] In Jesus' day those guardians were the members of the Sanhedrin, who had condemned Jesus. The leading priests and elders had ruled against Jesus in almost criminal fashion, violating much of their own protocol, yet they still saw themselves as having the law of Moses on their side—for God in Deuteronomy recognized their authority without reference to their own internal rules and protocol. This line of thought implied that if Jesus was the Messiah, then God himself had opposed the Sanhedrin. Further, he had dispensed with a key provision of his own Torah in validating Jesus as Messiah through his resurrection.

Simply put, if the claim that Jesus rose from the dead was true, Jesus must have been the Messiah (who else could he be?). It was commonly understood that through the Messiah the observance of Torah would be expanded worldwide. But had the very guardians of the Torah now condemned the Messiah? To a devout follower of the Torah law, this idea was blasphemous. It meant the keepers of Torah had essentially murdered the very one who embodied Israel's destiny, since the person of Messiah was the hope of Israel to one day live victoriously under Messiah's reign. This hope

---

35   1Co 1:22–23 is a reference to Jewish stumbling over precisely this issue.

36   There is independent documentation into the second century of this Jewish thinking and intransigence. See Justin, *Dialogue with Trypho*, 94, 96.

37   Dt 17:9–13; 21:5.

meant everything. Without a Messiah, the Jewish people did not have any certain future. Of course God would somehow be faithful to his promises, but Israel could hardly claim someone they had essentially murdered as their exclusive champion.

The idea that the Jews condemned their own Messiah for crucifixion would have—at least at first—shocked a simple, devout Jew. Crucifixion was stipulated only for the worst of criminals and the apostates who deserved God's wrath. The testimony of the early Christians was that Jesus died and rose again according to the Scriptures.[38] To the Greeks this resurrection faith was foolishness, but to the Jews it was a scandal,[39] because if the crucifixion of Jesus fulfilled their own Hebrew Scriptures—well, it was unthinkable! Thus, for the typical Jew committed to understanding and following Torah, the proclamation of "Christ crucified" was an outrageous claim that could only be true at the expense of turning their whole religious world upside-down.

To a Jew, to believe that Jesus was the Messiah because he rose from the dead meant the revelation that the Jews had—in effect— murdered God's champion and very possibly even fallen out of their privileged status as God's people.[40] At the very least, it required a whole new way of thinking about the future.

The Jews might have ignored the whole idea that Jesus' crucifixion meant much at all. But there was one problem. Jesus had not stayed in the grave.

---

38 1Co 15:3–4.

39 1Co 1:22–23.

40 Mt 21:43.

Third Point of Truth: A New View of Hebrew Prophecy

A. A crucified Messiah who rose again demands a reinterpretation of Jewish Messianic expectations.

B. The time of the fulfillment of God's end-time promises to Israel in Torah and the prophets has now arrived.

The third point of truth is established by the second point of truth. Here's how:

In the book of Deuteronomy one reads that priests of the Lord were chosen by God to minister and pronounce blessings in the name of the Lord and to decide all cases of dispute and assault.[41] The Torah of God authorized the priests to act as God's legal counsel. So the Sanhedrin authorities received their authority from the law of Moses, and that authority was not to be questioned. In fact, to seriously question their authority was tantamount to high treason.[42] They were using that authority when they indicted and convicted Jesus of blasphemy and high treason. Rome cooperated and the people agreed, but the Jewish authorities were the ones who really sentenced Jesus to death. But Jesus rose from the dead. This means that a crucified criminal has overturned the authority

---

41   Dt 17:8-10; 19:17-21.

42   Dt 17:9–13.

of the guardians of the Law Covenant of the Torah. According to the Hebrew Scriptures this is impossible—unless this man is truly the Messiah. But if this is true, then the Messiah's coming signals a future different than the one envisioned by their common understanding of Jewish prophecy.

Actually, Jesus had said something to this effect on the eve of his crucifixion. According to Jesus in his parable of the landowner, the Jewish leaders knew Jesus' true identity.[43] That they gave him to the Romans for crucifixion was the greater sin[44] and constituted rejection of the cornerstone of God's plan.[45] The result is that the very guardians of the Torah forfeited for the nation the opportunity to enter into the kingdom of God.[46] This was what Jesus said.

Again, a crucified Messiah—who was crucified, in effect by the guardians of Torah— demands a reevaluation of exclusive national Jewish privilege relative to the rest of humanity. This means, of course, that henceforth all prophecy given by the prophets of old would have to be reinterpreted, not just in light of Messiah's having come but in light of the fact that the one who embodied all the future promises of Israel had been rejected by the authorities who represented the nation. One needs to ask: How could Israel as a nation lay claim to a literal and national fulfillment of the promises of God to the seed of Abraham? God would still be true to his word, of course, but not exclusively through the nation of Israel. For although God committed himself to be faithful to his promises to the natural seed of Abraham, he had not promised to do so apart from his plan to bring to the world a whole new order of relationship and blessing through the Messiah. How

---

43   Mt 21:33–46; Mk 12:1–2; Lk 22:9–19.

44   Jn 19:11.

45   Mt 21:42.

46   Mt 21:43; Mt 8:11–12.

God would fulfill his promises to Israel remained to be seen and worked out in and through history.

So, again, a crucified Messiah who rose from the dead leads to a new way of looking at Israel's future—because the future has already arrived, so to speak, in the resurrection of the rejected Messiah.

In summary, Israel understood that at the end of time God would judge his people for acceptance or rejection.[47] The approved would enter into their reward. They would be raised from the dead into everlasting life. But the Messiah had come and had already been raised. So the resurrection of Jesus to eternal life meant Jesus had been accepted by God, and that the bar of God—the day of God's final verdict on whether or not to grant eternal life to individual humans—had been moved from the future *only* to the present *also*. The end-times foreseen by the Hebrew prophets[48] had arrived, though not in full, and not as anticipated. But God's end-time had been inaugurated and must therefore already be in process, in spite of Israel's untimely rejection of their Messiah. So now humanity lives in an in-between time—the time between Jesus' resurrection and the final resurrection of the dead at the very end of the end-times. The great delay of the fulfillment of God's blessings for the world is over, now that Jesus has risen from the dead.

---

47   Da 12:2–3.

48   1Pe 1:10–12.

Fourth Point of Truth: The Kingdom of God Has Come

A. Jesus' resurrection and ascension fulfills the prophetic word to David that his descendant would sit on his throne forever.

B. Jesus is Lord over a kingdom—one that functions from heaven but has invaded the earth.

The fourth point of truth derives directly from the third point of truth. The kingdom of God has arrived from the future—in a fashion and form unanticipated by Israel.

The kingdom of God has not arrived on Earth because God is sovereign king over all the earth. The kingdom of God has not arrived because Jesus came into the world. The kingdom of God was close at hand but had not yet arrived when John the Baptist and Jesus began their ministries. *The kingdom of God came only with the installation of the king on his imperial throne.*[49]

Where is the greatest revelation of the Christ to be found in the Hebrew Scriptures? Anyone who inquires into the writings of David in the Psalms, in the story of David, and especially in the prophecies to David and his seed will have an answer. Certainly one of the greatest revelations of Christ emerging from the whole

---

49   Ps 2:6–8; 110:11–6.

Old Testament is the proclamation that Messiah as the seed of David will reign over his Messianic kingdom. The kingdom of God could only come as and when the Messiah was installed as king on the throne of his father, David.[50]

And when might that be? On the day of Pentecost, Peter declares that David understood the promise of God, for God had promised "with an oath to him that of the fruit of his body, according to the flesh, he would raise up the Christ to sit on his throne."[51] Peter says David understood that God was talking about raising up Jesus from the dead: "He, foreseeing this, spoke concerning the resurrection of the Christ."[52] So Peter quotes David in the Psalms to prove that the resurrection of Christ was his installation on the throne of David. David's throne had been transferred to heaven, and Christ was raised up to David's throne when he was raised up from the dead to heaven.

The proclamation that Jesus is Lord has specific content. It means that Jesus is the Lord of whom David spoke when he wrote: "The Lord said to my Lord, 'Sit at my right hand till I make Your enemies Your footstool.' ... 'You are a priest forever according to the order of Melchizedek.'"[53] *Jesus is Lord* is the battle cry of the kingdom of God, proclaiming that King Jesus now reigns on David's throne from heaven. The fact that Jesus has risen means that the time of the fulfillment of God's end-time promises and the reign of God through Messiah has come. Jesus is Lord over a kingdom whose throne is in heaven, but now is in the process of invading Earth.

Peter preached this fourth point of truth on the day of Pentecost as central and foundational, because it summed up the gospel

---

50   Ps 89:3, 4, 34–37; Ps 110:1–3.

51   Ac 2:30.

52   Ac 2:31.

53   Ps 110:1, 4.

message. In a word, the kingdom of God has now come because from now on Jesus is king—because he conquered death and rose from the dead.

Fifth Point of Truth: The Worldwide Outpouring of Blessing

A. Jesus is the true descendant of Abraham who has received the promised blessing for the nations.

B. Jesus extends his kingdom everywhere by pouring out his Spirit.

This point follows from the fourth point, especially in the preaching of Peter on the day of Pentecost.

The pouring out of the Spirit was the sign that would inaugurate the new age of the Messiah. One of the things the Jews were looking forward to when the Messiah came was an outpouring of the Spirit of God. This outpouring would not just be for themselves but would extend out to the whole earth.

As Isaiah said, they awaited the time coming when "the Spirit [would be] poured upon us from on high, and the wilderness becomes a fruitful field, and the fruitful field is counted as a forest."[54]

They longed for the time when God would fulfill his word through Ezekiel: "I will give you a new heart and put a new spirit within

---

54   Isa 32:15.

you; I will take the heart of stone out of your flesh and give you a heart of flesh. I will put My Spirit within you and cause you to walk in My statutes, and you will keep My judgments and do them."[55]

Isaiah also declared: "The glory of the Lord shall be revealed, and all flesh shall see it together; for the mouth of the Lord has spoken."[56]

Then, again, Isaiah pulls back the curtain and allows us to overhear God speaking to his Servant, the Messiah: "Indeed, He says, 'It is too small a thing that You should be My servant to raise up the tribes of Jacob, and to restore the preserved ones of Israel; I will also give You as a light to the Gentiles, that You should be My salvation to the ends of the earth.'"[57]

While being careful to lay out the dominoes in proper order—so that I have yet to define salvation or to explore the connection between God's salvation and the blessing promised to the world through Abraham—one can still see that this passage clearly speaks about the blessing of God that will come to the nations through the Messiah.

Paul communicates this same idea by quoting the prophets also: "And again he says: 'Rejoice, O Gentiles, with His people!' And again: 'Praise the Lord, all you Gentiles! Laud Him, all you peoples!' ... 'In Him the Gentiles shall hope.'"[58]

Above all, perhaps, the Jews before Christ had the words of the prophecy of Joel: "And it shall come to pass afterward that I will pour out My Spirit on all flesh."[59] In fulfillment of this prophecy

---

55   Eze 36:26–27.

56   Isa 40:5.

57   Isa 49:6.

58   Ro 15:10-12, quoting Dt 32:43 and Ps 117:1.

59   Joel 2:28.

and many others, they expected that in the days of Messiah the nations also would come under both his rule and his blessings.

The idea that the nations would participate in the blessings of Abraham was clearly foretold by the prophets, notably Joel. The Jew living before the time of Christ regarded this prediction as established truth. On the day of Pentecost Peter assumed this knowledge and told his hearers that the events they were witnessing were positive proofs that the new age of Messiah had come.

This meant, of course, that Jesus was the true descendant, or seed of Abraham, who had received the power to bless the nations. For, as Peter exclaimed, after Jesus rose from the grave and ascended to heaven he "received from the Father the promise of the Holy Spirit."[60] In other words, he received within himself the fullness of the blessing that God had promised Abraham for the whole world. Jesus became a life-giving spirit.[61] At his ascension the Spirit of God became the Spirit of the Messiah, so that he could pour out that Spirit in fulfillment of the promise to Abraham that in his seed all the nations of the earth would be blessed.

---

60   Ac 2:33.

61   1Co 15:45.

Sixth Point of Truth: The End of the Law for Righteousness

A. As far as God's purposes are concerned, the time of the separation of the Jews and Gentiles is over.

B. Jesus' death has nullified the curse of the law and set the law aside as the way to God.

Since Pentecost, God had poured out his Spirit on Gentiles. The significance of this is that these Gentiles were people who did not obey those Torah laws that separated God's people from the other nations. Now a time in history has come when God himself has refused to make a distinction any longer between Torah observers and non-observers.[62] God's purposes are no longer separating Jew and Gentile into separate categories. The issue here is not whether to believe this, but how to understand it.

This sixth point of truth follows directly from the fifth point of truth and from the fact of God's sovereign action to bless the nations. Apparently, from God's point of view, no worldwide outpouring of God's Spirit in fulfillment of his end-time purposes would be expedient without a change in the relationship between God's chosen people and the other nations. Now it is revealed that God must have always intended from the time of promise to Abraham that his people should be a single family: that all

---

62   Ro 3:22; Gal 3:27–28; Col 3:11.

nations should be blessed in Abraham, and therefore, the one worldwide family of blessing could not be characterized by attempted obedience to the separating laws of Torah. That would have meant a plurality of families, with Jews and proselytes on the one hand and (believing) Gentiles on the other—and the Gentiles even further subdivided by their various races. The law's restriction on the ownership of the Abrahamic promises to Israel under Torah was a temporary measure introduced for specific purposes for a specific time period only. When Jesus rose from the dead, everything changed. This is what the author of Hebrews meant when he wrote, "For the priesthood being changed, of necessity there is also a change of the law."[63]

Through death and resurrection Jesus has broken down the middle wall of partition separating Jew and Gentile.[64] The worldwide outpouring of the Spirit does not distinguish between races, cultures or ancestry. As far as God's purposes are concerned, the time of separation of Jews and Gentiles is over. This means, at the very least, that any and all provisions of the law of Moses that separated Jew from Gentile are no longer valid. This was Paul's point when he said that we are "justified by faith apart from the deeds of the law"[65]—what a Jew does to be a Jew as distinct from a Gentile. Those binding restrictions, including the dietary laws, holy days, circumcision, and the entire Levitical system of sacrifices and offerings are no longer useful in this new era.

But how has this happened? Paul reveals that Jesus' death has nullified the curse of the law for this purpose—that the Abrahamic blessing of the outpouring of the Holy Spirit might come on the Gentiles.[66]

---

63   Heb 7:12.
64   Eph 2:14.
65   Ro 3:28.
66   Gal 3:8–14.

But did Jesus exhaust the curse by taking it on himself? That is the claim of some perspectives on Jesus' death. However, if that were true, the events of AD 70 and the destruction of Jerusalem would never have happened.[67]

According to Deuteronomy, the person hung on a cross was cursed—the curse was simply that of being hung on a cross to die.[68] That meant rejection and expulsion from the land of covenant and the inheritance of the covenant. On the cross Jesus was put out of the covenant inheritance. The guardians of the Torah were responsible for so cursing Jesus, and the Torah backed their decisions. This means the law covenant itself is implicated in Jesus' death. This means that in Jesus' resurrection he passed through and beyond the jurisdiction of the old covenant without reference to any of its requirements or restrictions.

That is good news because Christians are united with Christ by union with him in his death and resurrection.[69] Whatever benefits Jesus received through his death and resurrection believers receive. This means believers have passed through and beyond the jurisdiction of the law covenant, just as Paul testified.

> Therefore, my brethren, you also have become dead to the law through the body of Christ, that you may be married to another—to Him who was raised from the dead, that we should bear fruit to God. For when we were in the flesh, the sinful passions which were aroused by the law were at work in our members to bear fruit to death. But now we have been delivered from the law, having died to what we were held by, so that we should

---

67   See Mt 23:37–39. Insisting that the curse of the law of Moses against unfaithful Israel will be fully carried out, Jesus quotes Dt 32:11–12 in the Song of Moses, a song of God's righteous judgment.

68   Dt 21:23; Gal 3:13.

69   Ro 6:5.

> serve in the newness of the Spirit and not in the
> oldness of the letter.[70]

All those who identify with Christ in his death and resurrection
have passed through the curse of the law, and their future is with
Christ in his overcoming victory—a victory that includes triumph
over death itself. So in Christ, and only in Christ, the curse of
the law is nullified. Hence, all those in union with him cannot
be subjected to or bound by the restrictions of the old covenant,
and God's worldwide family of blessing is comprised of those
who have received the Spirit of the Messiah apart from the former
constraints of the law.

---

70   Ro 7:4–6.

Seventh Point of Truth: The Significance of the Cross

A. Because of the resurrection, the cross of Jesus was not a defeat but a victory.

B. The cross was the supreme occasion of God's mercy.

The seventh point rests on the six foundational points that preceded it, but especially the last three: now that the prophecies to David have been fulfilled by Christ (Point 4), now that the risen Jesus has been revealed as the fountainhead of God's blessings based on God's word to Abraham (Point 5), and now that Jesus' death has nullified the curse contained in the law and set it aside (Point 6), the cross gathers together these themes and becomes the symbol of victory and the focal point of God's forgiveness and mercy.

How would a first-century Jewish Christian make sense of this? How would he use his own Hebrew Scripture to reach beyond the familiar and grasp this new truth? The answer is in the concept of covenant. Christ climaxes each of the major Old Testament covenants: the Davidic covenant (Point 4), the Abrahamic covenant (Point 5), and the Mosaic covenant (Point 6).

Consider first the prophetic word to David (Point 4) and the emphasis on it in the book of Acts as it records the first proclamations of the gospel. God had said to David that he would make an everlasting covenant with him, called the "sure mercies of David."[71] That Davidic covenant included many specific dimensions of blessings but especially God's provision of mercy. David's seed could fail miserably, but God would never take his loving kindness from them.[72] The covenant promises also declared that through David's seed his throne would be established forever.[73] But these prophecies of kingdom dominion have been fulfilled in Christ (Point 4), and the promised blessings of mercy must follow. So in his missionary journeys, Paul declared, concerning Jesus, "that through this Man is preached to you the forgiveness of sins."[74] When Paul said that, he was talking specifically about "the sure mercies of David" as the immediate outcome of the fact that God raised up Jesus.

> And we declare to you glad tidings—that promise which was made to the Fathers. God has fulfilled this for us their children, in that He has raised up Jesus. As it is also written in the second Psalm: "You are My Son, today I have begotten You." And that He raised Him from the dead, no more to return to corruption, He has spoken thus: "I will give you the sure mercies of David" … Therefore let it be known to you, brethren, that through this Man is preached to you the forgiveness of sins; and by Him everyone who believes is justified from all things from which you could not be justified by the law of Moses.[75]

So the forgiveness of sins comes to God's people through the risen Lord Jesus, they are the sure mercies of David, and they do something that the law of Moses could not do.

---

71   Isa 55:3.

72   2Sa 7:15; Ps 89:20–37.

73   2Sa 7:16; Ps 89:29, 36–27.

74   Ac 13:38.

75   Ac 13:32–34, 38, 39.

The word of the gospel, simply put here, is that Jesus is risen, he is Lord, and he grants forgiveness[76] through the mercies of David that flow through him from the Father. This simple perspective is predicated upon the fact and significance of the resurrection. As Paul put it, Jesus' death on the cross did nothing without the resurrection. "And if Christ is not risen, your faith is futile; you are still in your sins!"[77]

No first-century believer ever remotely imagined that the cross atoned for sins apart from Jesus' rising from the dead. But with the resurrection, wow! Because of the resurrection, the cross turns everything upside down. The death of Jesus at the hands of the Romans becomes not a defeat but a victory, because in the end he conquered. He overcame all Israel's enemies, whether the Romans, the guardians of the Torah (!), or sin and death itself. "Having disarmed principalities and powers, He made a public spectacle of them, triumphing over them in [the cross]."[78] In light of the resurrection the cross of Jesus was a victory over all humanity's real foes—sin, death, the curse of the law of Moses, and every principality and power of Satan. That's because through faith in Jesus Christians are united with him in his death so that when he rose they rose with him.

> For if we have been united together in the likeness of His death, certainly we also shall be in the likeness of His resurrection, knowing this, that our old man was crucified with Him, that the body of sin might be done away with, that we should no longer be slaves of sin. For he who has died has been freed from sin. Now if we died with Christ, we believe that we shall also live with Him, knowing that Christ, having been raised

---

76 See also Ac 5:31.

77 1Co 15:17.

78 Col 2:15.

from the dead, dies no more. Death no longer has dominion over Him.[79]

... buried with Him in baptism, in which you also were raised with Him through faith in the working of God, who raised Him from the dead.[80]

Along with great victory belong celebration and great magnanimous gestures. With the Davidic covenant now fulfilled, Jesus' death on the cross becomes the supreme occasion for the mercy of God.

How does this work? One truth stands out, a perspective on the cross and with it the forgiveness of sins. Once again, the idea of covenant gives perspective. Paul declares "by Him everyone who believes is justified from all things from which you could not be justified by the law of Moses."[81] The great thing for the Christian is how superior is God's provision in Christ over the law of Moses. The author of Hebrews wrote that Christ died as "the Mediator of the new covenant, by means of death,"[82] "bringing a "change of the law."[83]

Paul says, "For I through the law died to the law that I might live to God ... I do not set aside the grace of God; for if righteousness comes through the law, then Christ died in vain."[84]

If the death of Christ meant anything, it meant the end of the law of Moses for right standing with God. To say it another way, there can be no thought of Jesus and *atonement* without this underlying foundation. Whenever one affirms that "Christ died

---

79   Ro 6:5–9.

80   Col 2:12.

81   Ac 13:39.

82   Heb 9:15.

83   Heb 7:12.

84   Gal 2:19, 21. In the original gospel, the way the cross functions to grant justification is to set aside the law as a means of righteousness, thus releasing God's forgiveness to those who embrace the Messiah.

for our sins" one is declaring freedom from the necessity to obey the law covenant of Moses, even when one does not state this idea outright. If this is not true, Christ died in vain.

When it came to the issue of the forgiveness of sins, God could not just decide to forgive and let it go at that. No, God had made covenant with his people, the law covenant of Moses. It mediated the terms of forgiveness. Its curse fell on all who spurned the covenant itself,[85] and in the end, that included Israel as a whole.[86] It had become an obstacle to the ongoing purposes of God. So what did Jesus do? He became subjected to the curse when he was crucified, and he died as one cursed by the law.[87] The curse was never removed, but those who have passed through it are no longer subjected to it. If anyone identifies with Jesus in his death and resurrection, then his death to the law becomes that person's death to the law as well.

> Or do you not know, brethren (for I speak to those who know the law), that the law has dominion over a man as long as he lives? ... Therefore, my brethren, you also have become dead to the law through the body of Christ, that you may be married to another—to Him who was raised from the dead, that we should bear fruit to God ... But now we have been delivered from the law, having died to what we were held by, so that we should serve in the newness of the Spirit and not in the oldness of the letter.[88]

Christians have died to the law and passed out from its domain; it has no hold on them, and God, through Jesus, has freely granted to them new life in the Spirit, and, along with it, forgiveness based

---

85   Dt 27:26.

86   Mt 23:37, 38; Heb 8:7–8; Dt 27–28; Lev 26:14–39; Gal 3:10–13.

87   Gal 3:13.

88   Ro 7:1, 4, 6.

on the tender mercies guaranteed to us through the covenant with David.

When Jesus rose from the dead he fulfilled God's promise to David that his seed would sit on his throne, releasing "the sure mercies of David" to God's people (i.e., the forgiveness of sins)[89] but the cross was essential[90] because through sin the law stood in the way. True freedom could only come by death, but it needed to be a specific kind of death—death due to the law's curse. That required the cross. By crucifixion the requirements of Torah were fulfilled—in the resurrection—establishing Jesus as God's final authority to forgive whomever he chooses.

Now the Bible statement, "Jesus died for our sins" can be clearly understood. *He died so that every human being, by identification, could die with him as one cursed by the law, so that in being raised with him he would pass from the law's domain and could receive the forgiveness of sins that has been freely granted.* "Christ died for us."[91]

The Scriptures occasionally refer to Jesus' death as a sin-offering like that offered in the temple under the old covenant. Animal sacrifices had been instituted that Israel might learn the ways of God. They demonstrated the contrite heart of the Israelite who offered the sacrifice. When the Jews began to think of the sacrifices in merely legal terms, as paying a penalty, Isaiah and the other prophets sharply rebuked them, insisting the only acceptable sacrifice was one offered by a covenant-keeping Jew who was

---

89   Isa 55:3–4; Ac 13:34.

90   One mystery of the Davidic covenant has been that God said of the true seed of David, "If he commits iniquity, I will chasten him… but my mercy shall not depart from him" (2Sa 7:14–15). How could this possibly apply to Jesus? Well, it applies to believers. Those who identify with him are counted as in him and regarded as though they are him. Ps 89:30–32 clarifies this point.

91   Ro 8:32; Eph 5:2; Ro 5:6. The Greek word *huper* means "on our behalf." See also Gal 1:4 and 1Co 11:24.

confessing and repenting of sin.[92] Proverbs insists that in mercy and truth atonement is provided for iniquity[93] because, in the end, God is looking for a right heart and not a sin-offering.[94]

If one thinks of Jesus' death like an Old Testament sacrifice for sins, one needs to remember again that only the truly penitent sinner could offer an acceptable sacrifice.[95] Believers who need forgiveness of sin confess their sin and are forgiven, but the sacrifice which they offer is the one sacrifice offered once for all time.[96] In this sense, Jesus is the sacrifice for sin, dispensing his grace to his people because the new order of Messiah—his kingdom of grace and mercy—has been forever established.

Finally, any understanding of the significance of the cross should be built primarily on the knowledge that God's objective in Christ was to channel his grace and mercy to humanity. Common is the thought that God needed to be reconciled to humanity, and, yet, Christ's death on the cross was intended to bring to death any old or defective way of looking at the problem of sin. Scripture does not actually record anywhere that redemption was necessary because God needed to be reconciled to humanity.[97] It does say humanity needed to be reconciled to him. "God was in Christ reconciling the world to Himself, not imputing their trespasses to them."[98] The death of Jesus was the supreme occasion of God's mercy, declaring that God has reconciled his people to himself.[99]

---

92   Ps 51:16–19; Isa 1:13–20; Mal 2:13–14.

93   Pro 16:6.

94   Ps 50:7–21; Ps 51:16–17; Mic 6:6–8.

95   Ps 51:19; Lev 4:22–28; Num 15:30–31; Isa 1:10–20; Jer 7:22–23; Hos 6:6; Mic 6:6–8.

96   Heb 10:12; Rev 5:6.

97   What can be stated via linguistic studies may or may not be another story but doesn't concern us here.

98   2Co. 5:19.

99   2Co 5:18–21; Ro 5:10–11; Eph 2:16; Col 1:20.

Whatever else one may affirm, understanding God's merciful intention should remain paramount.

If one seeks the original first-century gospel, and so confines oneself to the actual statements of Scripture, then the peace made possible with God would not be because Jesus' death appeased God.[100] Rather, the Spirit of Christ has made known God's mercy and grace. In this new time in history, inaugurated by the resurrection of Jesus, God opens wide his heart to the entire human race, awaiting the response to the good news from every person.

---

100   All arguments to the contrary center on the meaning of the Greek word for propitiation in Ro 3:25. From Homer on, the verb related to this noun meant to placate an offended individual or an angry God. But scriptural terms must derive their meanings from scriptural context, not from pagan sources. No direct New Testament evidence exists that this word is ever used to refer to appeasing God. In the traditional Greek sense, the whole idea of propitiating God is unscriptural. It plays havoc with the Bible's fundamental tenet that God himself acted first to solve humanity's dilemma. God took action in Christ at the very beginning (Rev 13:8b). Scripture asserts the truth of the divine initiative when it uses the word propitiation (1Jn 4:10; Ro 3:24–25). I offer this extended footnote because my assertion runs counter to the much beloved evangelical atonement theory that Jesus suffered the wrath of almighty God for the sin of God's people, taking their place on the cross. This is not the place to debate this doctrine, and I make no case here one way or the other. But I emphasize my point that penal substitutionary atonement, true or not, was not original church teaching. In fact, it was not taught in the church for the first fifteen hundred years of its existence. (John Calvin created it as an improvement on Anselm's atonement theory.) It, like other atonement theories, emerged only after the *original resurrection perspective* of the gospel had been lost. The original gospel did not even need any atonement theory—that is, none other than what Paul wrote hidden in plain view!

Eighth Point of Truth: The New Covenant Established

A. Jesus died and rose again to establish the new covenant.

B. The new covenant is the charter of the kingdom of God, fulfilling and thus superseding all previous covenants God made with Israel.

This eighth point expands the seventh, helps explain it, and follows immediately from the sixth and seventh points.

Jesus died and rose again for this purpose—that he might establish the new covenant. However, it was when Jesus rose from the dead, not before, that he actually established the covenant. This is clearly stated in Hebrews in the actual Greek: "But the God of peace, he that led up from among the dead the great Shepherd of the sheep—with the blood of an everlasting covenant—our Lord Jesus …"[101] The author of Hebrews declares that the blood of the covenant itself arose into its destined place with Jesus when he arose from the dead. Jesus was the mediator of the new covenant by means of death, signifying that through death—all the way through death to the resurrection—believers have been granted the remission of their offenses.

101　Heb 13:20. This verse looks back on the whole book of Hebrews, where the great high priest of the new covenant is really the risen Christ playing the key role in our redemption (Heb 2:17-3:2; 4:14-15; 5:5-10; 6:20; 7:11-17, 20-27; 8:1-2, 6; 9:11-12, 23-28; 10:12-14, 21).

Up ahead, the Eleventh Point of Truth will explore what it means to be saved. At this point, however, it still might be helpful to note the importance of Christ's resurrection concerning salvation. "For if when we were enemies we were reconciled to God through the death of His Son, much more, having been reconciled, we shall be saved by His [resurrection] life."[102] Paul taught that "if Christ is not risen, your faith is futile; you are still in your sins!"[103] The resurrection of Christ was not merely the happy outcome of the cross. *The resurrection was that key event without which we would still be lost in sins and without any new covenant established.*

So through Jesus' death and his resurrection, Christians enjoy a new covenant prophesied by the prophets of old. The bottom-line of that covenant is, "I will forgive their iniquity, and their sin I will remember no more."[104] The forgiveness of sins obtained by Christ is covenantal in nature. By his death one covenant is fulfilled and left behind, and by his death and resurrection another covenant is established. Hence believers have freedom from the law, that is, the old covenant. References to Jesus' death for sins are statements to this effect—usually from the point of view that Jesus replaces the temple sacrifices. *Such statements may be regarded as Bible shorthand notation for the entire benefits of the new covenant.*

The prophets, especially Jeremiah, had foretold the coming of a new covenant to Israel and Judah.[105] On the eve of his death Jesus told his disciples that he was initiating this new covenant through the shedding of his blood.[106] At that time Jesus spoke of the arrival of the kingdom of God and this new covenant.[107] In effect, he declared the new covenant to be the charter of the

---

102   Ro 5:10.

103   1Co 15:17.

104   Jer 31:34.

105   Jer 31:31–34.

106   Mt 26:28; Mk 14:24; Lk 22:20; 1Co 11:25.

107   Mt 26:29; Mk 14:25; Lk 22:18.

coming kingdom of God. But the kingdom could not arrive until the installation of the King, and that required Jesus' death and resurrection to establish the covenant itself.

The distinction of the new covenant is that God will put his laws in the mind and write them on the heart.[108] God's laws, written in stone, were given at the first Jewish Pentecost at Sinai. Now, for the Christian, God writes them in minds and hearts with the activity of the Holy Spirit. In other words, the intent of the new covenant is accomplished by the pouring out of the Spirit into the human heart—exactly what the prophets foretold. The result of the new covenant is the gift of the Spirit so that the righteous requirement of the law is fulfilled through the Spirit.[109]

So, for Christians, the new covenant of Jeremiah 31 was proclaimed by Jesus through the Last Supper, was inaugurated at his resurrection through his blood, and was fulfilled in Pentecost with the coming of the Holy Spirit.

This fulfillment of the law's intent is exactly what Torah declared the kingdom of God to be all about. So the kingdom of God has come.

The defining charter of the kingdom of God is the new covenant, and the operative power of the covenant is the Spirit of Messiah poured out from on high, from the exalted throne of that kingdom.

As seen earlier in the fourth and fifth points of truth, Jesus is the true seed of David and the true seed of Abraham. This means that the new covenant fulfills the covenants God made with David and with Abraham. Simply put, *the new covenant is nothing more or less than the Davidic covenant fulfilled by Christ, and then extended to all those who, by faith, belong to him* (Points 4 and 5). In exactly

---

108   Jer 31:33.

109   Ro 8:3–4.

the same way, of course, *the new covenant is the fulfillment of the Abrahamic covenant* (Point 5).[110]

The new covenant gathers into itself all the promises by covenant that God made with Israel so that they are all fulfilled in and through Jesus. This is what Paul meant when he wrote, "Jesus Christ has become a servant to the circumcision for the truth of God, to confirm the promises made to the fathers, and that the Gentiles might glorify God for His mercy."[111] The first Christians agreed with Paul, that "all the promises of God in Him are Yes, and in Him Amen."[112]

---

110   Gal 3:16, 29.

111   Ro 15:8–9.

112   2Co 1:20.

Ninth Point of Truth: Jesus as Adam's Replacement

A. The new covenant reaches all the way back to Adam in its scope.

B. Jesus is Adam's true replacement; he succeeds where Adam failed, and he cancels the curse of death.

It is time now to explore Israel's relation to Adam in view of the fall. This investigation sets the stage for an expanded view of Jesus and the scope, significance, and purpose of the new covenant. Then, this ninth point follows immediately from the points preceding, especially the eighth.

The story of God and humanity begins with Adam.[113] According to Paul the apostle, Adam was "a type of Him who was to come."[114] Almost no other biblical figure is so declared in Scripture—as a type of Christ.[115] Flawless in his original creation, created in the image of God,[116] Adam was given the mandate to rule and have dominion[117]—at least over the natural order of earth's created

---

113   Consider all mention of Adam as inclusive of Eve as well. See Ge 5:2.

114   Ro 5:14.

115   Melchisedek is the other possibility. Heb 5:6, 10; 6:20-7:1.

116   Ge 1:26, 27; 5:1.

117   Ge 1:26–28.

living beings, if not all of creation.[118] Then Adam was tempted to grasp at the special privilege of being like God.[119] He failed the test miserably.[120] Adam's disobedience set the general pattern of disobedience for the human race.[121] More to the point, Adam's failure resulted in the sentence of death on all humanity.[122]

As the Hebrew Scriptures unfold the story of humanity, the spotlight moves from Adam to Abraham and then to Abraham's descendants, the nation of Israel. The Israelites knew from their Torah that the fall of Adam in the garden had precipitated disastrous consequences, with sin and death reigning over humans ever since. They knew God had promised the seed of Abraham as a source of blessing to the world. They focused on God's word to their patriarch Abraham concerning them and their uniqueness in God's plan. What they did not understand was that God's answer to the human condition was contained in his original promise to Abraham. They did not see the overarching meaning of God's promises to Abraham because they failed to see themselves properly in the scheme of things. They did not see the necessity of their failure in order that grace might come into focus.[123]

So Israel, like Adam, failed miserably. Like Adam, they were kicked out of their "garden" (the Promised Land). In the whole process—and through their exile—they revealed once again the sentence that was pronounced upon humanity in the garden, the sentence of death. Human mortality—that sentence of death—has its source in sin, and the Torah was given to Israel in order that we—all of humanity—might see our sin and our desperate

---

118   See Heb 2:6–8.

119   Ge 3:1–5.

120   Ge 3:6-7.

121   Ro 5:15–21.

122   Ge 3:17–19, Ro 5:15, 17, 21.

123   See Paul's extended argument in Ro 9–11.

need for a new era of grace through a new covenant (Point 8).[124] How was God to address the real problem and not merely prop up Israel?

When God made promises to Abraham, he had something much bigger in mind than simply creating a nation of people, giving them a promised land, and using them in some vague way to bless the Gentiles. Israel and her failure in relation to the law covenant was a mirror, provided so human beings might see their true plight in order that the universal sentence of death on the human race might come into focus, paving the way for a whole new order of life and blessing.

Abraham, then, was much more than the beginning of the history of a particular people in the earth. Abraham was the beginning of the answer to the fall of Adam and the plight of human beings who are subject to sin and death. But God's actual answer to the need was Jesus, the seed of David, and the seed of Abraham (Points 4 and 5). What this means is that the new covenant, as God's response to our human situation, reaches back not only to Abraham—to make Jesus the true seed of Abraham—but all the way back to Adam to make Jesus the true new Adam, the son of Adam who overcame where the original Adam failed.

One can see this best by focusing briefly on how Jesus succeeded where Adam failed:

- Adam was created in the image of God. Jesus was the express image of the Father.[125]

- Adam was flawless in his original creation. Jesus was without sin in birth and in life.[126]

---

124   Ro 5:20; 7:7–8, 13.

125   2Co 4:4, Col 1:15, Heb 1:3.

126   1Pe 2:22, Heb. 4:15; 7:26.

- Adam was given the mandate to rule over creation. In like manner, before his crucifixion, Jesus at times exercised dominion over nature, as we see in his commanding the wind and waves to be still.[127]

- Adam was tempted to grasp at the special privilege of being like God, and so was Jesus.[128]

- Adam miserably failed the one test and walked away from God.[129] Jesus succeeded at every test,[130] passed the final test of obedience to the Father,[131] and committed his spirit to God.[132]

- Adam's disobedience set the general pattern of disobedience for the human race. Jesus set the pattern of obedience, and by his obedience many would be made righteous.[133]

- Adam's failure resulted in the sentence of death on all humanity. Jesus has reversed the sentence of death and brought life and immortality.[134]

In light of his triumph, Jesus could now be seen as the fulfillment of the ancient Hebrew prophecy of God's response to remedy the fall.[135] This means that Jesus, the true seed of Abraham, is also the true son of Adam, the completion of Adam, the last Adam

---

127   Mt 8:23–27; Mk 4:35–41; Lk 8:22–25.

128   Php 2:5–8.

129   Ge 3:8.

130   Heb 2:5–18; 4:15.

131   Php 2:8.

132   Lk 23:48.

133   Ro 5:19.

134   Ro 5:18, 21.

135   Ge 3:15.

needed. As such, he becomes Adam's replacement, the key to the human race and the second man from heaven.[136]

Christ's death answers the curse contained in the law, effectively nullifying that curse and releasing the promised blessing for those who identify with Christ in his death and resurrection (Point 6).[137] But Christ's resurrection into immortal life means that far more than just the curse of the law was canceled. For death itself has been defeated,[138] and the curse of death has therefore been canceled. The sentence of death given in the garden to Adam and his posterity no longer has any hold on those who belong to Christ.[139] They have effectively passed through the drama of death and into the eternal life beyond.[140] By what means has this happened? By means of relationship with Messiah, the sentence of death is reversed. By being identified with him in death, believers in Messiah are assured a similar future of eternal life.[141] In so overcoming, Jesus, as the second man and Adam's replacement, undoes the original curse.

Just as all those who are incorporated into the original Adam are subjected to sin and the consequent sentence of death imposed in the garden, even so, all those who are incorporated into the "new Adam" have effectively passed through the sentence of death into life beyond death, the everlasting resurrection life.

Early on, the first Christians[142] received this expanded Messianic perspective of the two Adams (Adam and Jesus). They obviously

---

136   1Co 15:47.

137   Gal 3:8–14.

138   Ro 5:12–21; 6:9; 1Co 15:26, 54–57.

139   2Ti 1:10; 1Co 15:57; Ro 8:32;8:16.

140   Heb 2:14–15; Jn 5:24.

141   Ro 6:5.

142   Was this teaching on Adam and Jesus unique to Paul? Many scholars are convinced this kind of thinking about Christ and Adam was widespread before Paul even wrote his letters.

did so in the process of paying attention to the Hebrew Scriptures in light of the revelation of the Holy Spirit on the new covenant (Point 8). They must have realized that their new perspective was significant, perhaps key, to their grasp of the gospel. In it Jesus' humanity was in full view. But Jesus was more than just a mere human, he was the federal head of the renewed human race—the head of the new creation.

This perspective, of course, is impossible without the early church emphasis on the resurrection. Once again, the resurrection opens windows to truth, and the revelation of its significance unfolds the meaning of the gospel.

Tenth Point of Truth: Change in Time and History

A. The risen Messiah created a new future for Israel, those who belong to Jesus, the human race, and the entire universe.

B. People today are living in a new in-between time in history, when Messiah reigns in the midst of his enemies until his return.

This point follows from points 3, 4, 5, 6, 8 and 9.

The time of the fulfillment of God's end-time promises to Israel has arrived (Point 3). Jesus' resurrection and ascension fulfill the prophetic word to David that his seed would sit on his throne forever (Point 4). The kingdom of God has come, and the worldwide outpouring of blessing has commenced, as prophesied (Point 5). The time of separation of Jews and Gentiles is over (Point 6). We are now in the time of the new covenant (Point 8). Jesus has replaced Adam as the true progenitor of the people of God's favor (Point 9).

Each of the above statements underscores the now-obvious summary truth that the resurrection of Jesus has created a new future for Israel, for those who belong to Jesus, for the entire human race, and for the very cosmos itself.

Furthermore, what Israel initially expected to happen when Messiah came had been based on the typical Hebrew timeline of history. The original idea was that history itself was a succession of ages, one after the other, moving forward and never repeating. There was a beginning point (creation) and an ending point (the final judgment). This succession of many ages could be divided into two periods. The first period was to succeed the other according to God's predetermined plan. At that time, God would put to right the failures and sufferings of the past and the present age in the coming of the new age. The Messiah was the key to everything. He was to be God's instrument to make this change happen. He was supposed to climax the old age and to inaugurate this new messianic age, which was to be the time of blessing and utopia that God had promised his people.

But notice what happened. The Messiah's actual coming required this understanding to be modified. To be sure, right now Messiah reigns from heaven. He "has gone into heaven and is at the right hand of God, angels, and authorities and powers having been made subject to Him."[143] He reigns until all his enemies are put under his feet.[144] His coming and resurrection were indeed at the climax, the fullness of time.[145] But it is evident that the final end did not come at that time, because the dead were not raised and the judgment did not take place. So the climax was incomplete, and Christ, who had already come, must yet fulfill the rest of the Hebrew prophetic picture. So he must come again! And only in that way would the rest of the final events unfold.

The anticipated reign of Messiah was to be the end of history, but his first coming has become the midpoint of history, revealing a new development in the story of Israel and the whole human race.

---

143   1Pe 3:22.

144   Ps 110:1; Da 2:44; Mt 22:44; Mk 12:36; Lk 20:42–43; Ac 2:34–35; Heb 1:13; 10:13.

145   Gal 4:4; Heb 1:2; Eph 1:10; 1Pe 1:20; 2Pe 3:3; 1 Jn 2:18; Jude 18.

The key point here is that when Christ came the first time and did not fulfill everything immediately, he opened up a gap in the former Hebrew concept of time, beginning with Christ's resurrection. In this gap the two ages of anticipation and fulfillment run simultaneously. They will do so until the second coming of the Messiah.

This means that believers live in the overlap of the two ages, between the times. Messiah reigns in believers' hearts, and they are the initial expression and manifestation of that kingdom of Messiah to come, which is going to cover the whole earth.

Also, individual believers in Messiah are meant to view their history and destiny with an understanding of the overlap of the two ages. Just as history has an overlapping timeline so that history begins, arrives later at Messiah's first coming, and climaxes to an end still later, even so, individuals are born, then (perhaps) join themselves to Messiah, and still later—after death (for now)—climax their personal history at the judgment seat of Christ. Just as history is a process leading to a final end, one's personal history is a process that begins with allegiance to the Messiah and culminates in that person's final destiny. In other words, allegiance to Messiah implies a process that has a beginning, an in-between time, and an end-time. One could say the Messiah offers individuals a life of meaning and destiny that includes the past, the present, and the future.

Being joined to the Messiah marks the beginning, living for Messiah designates an in-between time, and one's final destiny and eternal future will be completed when Messiah returns. So Messiah reigns in the midst of his enemies until his return, and individual believers in Messiah live in the overlap of the two ages until that event.

Messiah has come, his decisive death has been offered, and he has risen. The believer in Messiah has responded to him so as to be included in the company of people who receive the deliverance he offers those who identify with him. So, in one sense, Messiah's action on behalf of the one who believes in him is already complete. It is past tense.

But in another sense, Messiah's benefits are up ahead as a predestined future, and that future cannot be considered complete until the verdict is given at the judgment seat of Christ. In that sense, then, the person who is now living his or her life for the Messiah has not yet arrived. Something is future!

The full benefits of Messiah's death, resurrection, and ascension—whether corporate or for the individual—are past, present, and future—all three. It just depends upon how one looks at it. The first Christians—fully informed by their resurrection faith—carried this perspective of change in time and history.

Eleventh Point of Truth: The Core Meaning of Salvation

A. The resurrection of Jesus is the foundation and real explanation of the salvation he offers.

B. The redemption of the body is the bedrock meaning of eternal life.

The point before last explored Jesus' identity in relation to Adam. Prior to the fall, Adam had life in the garden without the harsh reality of death, but he forfeited that privilege in the fall. Humanity—as the descendants of Adam—had to remain under the sentence of death unless and until that forfeiture could be overturned. This insight regarding Jesus' identity as the new Adam (Point 9), together with the understanding of the new covenant changes in time and history (Point 10), leads to the eleventh point of truth. *The resurrection of Jesus is not only the basis of all human hope for eternal life, it points to the way one should understand eternal life itself.*

Throughout Israel's history, the way God *saved* his people was by delivering them from their troubles, including from other nations—like the Philistines—or from famine or pestilence or whatever might destroy them, drive them out of their land, or oppress them.[146] *Salvation* always meant deliverance from

---

146   Ex 15:2; 2Sa 22:2; 1Ch 16:35; Ps 3:8; 7:1; 27:1; 31:2; 59:2; 68:20; 69:14; 71:4; 140:1.

something or someone that would oppress, harm, or destroy. The people of Israel understood that God had covenanted with them to save them, and their salvation was holistic, concrete, and this-worldly. In other words, their salvation was to be experienced in time and space—according to the way they understood the terms of their covenant, and was not relegated to an afterlife or some ethereal spiritual dimension. Old Testament salvation for them was about God's activity on behalf of his people to give them fullness of life and blessing in their land of promise.

When David, as a psalmist, extols God for his own individual experience of salvation, he generally refers to being rescued from the threat of premature physical death,[147] not the physical death that naturally completes a long and full life.[148]

But the Hebrew understanding did not remain static. As time passed, the Old Testament prophets began to declare God's faithfulness to Israel with a new clarity, especially in view of their exile from the land of promise. God was going to grant Israel a salvation that would be forever, that would never again be interrupted.[149] The God of Israel was a God of life and blessing, and the ultimate victory of the God of life would be uninterrupted life and blessing. If the blessing were to be lost, the victory would be forfeit. So the whole idea of salvation had to come up to a new level of meaning to square with an exalted view of God in light of the new reality of exile and restoration.

The idea of salvation as rescue from death developed into the understanding that God's final salvation must confer upon the

---

147 Ps 3:7–8; 6:4–10; 7:1–2, 10; 13:7:17:7; 18:3–6, 16–19, 27, 35, 46.

148 But sometimes David's cry for help reaches past this life and into the resurrection reality, which is just what you would expect from the principal person of the Old Testament foreshadowing Messiah. Ps 17:13–15; 16:9–11.

149 Isa 45:17; 51:6; Da 9:24.

individual recipient some kind of embodied, *everlasting* life. By the time of Daniel, the Hebrews had made that step.[150]

In quick summary, by the time of Jesus, to have the hope of life eternal meant something more than just being a wisp of smoke in an ethereal heaven. For the Israelites, with their understanding guided by their ancient writings, it came to imply humans being raised from the dead. This was the biblical and ancient Hebrew hope possessed by the Jews of Jesus' day. Many believed in the bodily resurrection of the dead, and at least the Pharisees insisted upon it as a defining tenet of their community.[151] According to the prophets there was to be a future resurrection for the faithful in Israel, for this was the only way God could be totally faithful to his covenant promises.[152] Jesus came on the scene functioning as a Jewish rabbi within the Hebrew culture, confirming the basic doctrine of the Pharisees about the resurrection.[153] After Jesus rose from the dead and commissioned his disciples, the gospel message they trumpeted set forth God's faithfulness in a startling new way. God had confirmed his faithfulness to his people by raising the Messiah from the dead into bodily, everlasting life.[154]

The Christian claim is that through resurrection Jesus gained something amazing, and he now offers that something to anyone. Again, what qualifies Jesus as Savior is that he arose in body from the dead. The purpose of Jesus' death was his resurrection[155] so that whoever is united with him might attain salvation.

What kind of salvation is that? Look at the original, biblical evidence.

---

150   Daniel 12 is a clear prediction of resurrection into everlasting life.

151   Ac 23:8.

152   Da 12:2–3; Job 19:25–26; Isa 26:19; Ps. 49:14–15; Eze 37:11–14.

153   Mt 22:23–32; Mk 12:18–27; Lk 20:27–40.

154   Ac 2:24, 30, 32; 3:15, 26; 4:10, 33; 5;30; 10:40; 13:23, 30, 33, 37; 17:31; 23:6; 26:8, 23.

155   Ro 6:4–6.

Paul is our earliest source for the Christian faith. He confessed himself to have been a "Hebrew of the Hebrews,"[156] and he writes on the same trajectory as the Hebrew, so that ultimately, for him, salvation must be holistic, concrete, and bodily. For example, when Paul writes to his converts in Thessalonica of "the hope of salvation," he is talking about "salvation [to be obtained] through our Lord Jesus Christ, who died for us, that whether we wake or sleep, we should live together with Him."[157] For Paul, the expectation of this salvation at Christ's future coming distinguishes believers from those "who have no hope"[158] of this afterlife. Bodily salvation is implied.

Then, when Paul writes to the Philippians, he tells them that the goal of Paul's faith in Christ is to "attain to the resurrection from the dead."[159] When the risen Lord returns he "will transform our lowly body that it may be conformed to His glorious body, according to the working [of resurrection power] by which He is able even to subdue all things to himself"[160]—even mortality and death. Here too salvation is bodily, embracing a future event whereby one's personal identity will be transformed into the bodily existence into which Christ was raised.

The book of 1 Corinthians contains the apostle's most lengthy and explicit definition of his gospel and the salvation it proclaims. Here he defines the gospel by which believers *are being saved*[161] as founded completely on Christ's resurrection from the dead.[162] He reasons from the reality of the risen Christ to the destiny of believers. He declares that at the coming of Christ, death will be

---

156 Php 3:5.

157 1Th 5:8–10.

158 1Th 4:13.

159 Php 3:8–11.

160 Php 3:21.

161 This is the literal Greek for "are saved" in 1Co 15:2.

162 1Co 15:1–11.

annihilated. The predicament of Adam's race is that the physical body is mortal, being of earthly origin. "Flesh and blood cannot inherit the kingdom of God; nor does corruption [i.e., a rotting corpse] inherit incorruption."[163] But at Christ's coming, all those living and dead who belong to Christ will be bodily transformed to his immortal existence. Thus, death and the power of moral evil will be forever vanquished and human destiny will be fulfilled.[164] Humanity's problem is at least a bodily issue, and the solution Paul's gospel proclaims is at least a bodily salvation.

The same perspective of bodily salvation underlies Paul's arguments in Romans. Paul reasons that "if the Spirit of [God] who raised Jesus from the dead dwells in you, He who raised Christ from the dead will also give life to your mortal bodies through His Spirit who dwells in you."[165] Paul is talking the language of bodily salvation.[166]

So to answer the question, "What kind of salvation is that?," the biblical answer is that the new covenant understanding is on the same trajectory as the Hebrew point of view. It points toward a salvation that is holistic and inclusive in its nature. The fullness of salvation declared in Jesus' resurrection must include bodily salvation,[167] the embodied life of the resurrection. *This is true not because salvation is confined to the realm of the body but because the body is the means by which the fullness of salvation is meant to be experienced.*

---

163   1Co 15:50.

164   1Co 15:20–28, 42–57.

165   Ro 8:11.

166   Paul's use of *eternal life* and *everlasting life* always reflects his Hebrew heritage—even when he exhorts believers to "lay hold on" the life of the age to come by the way they live their lives now (Ro 8:13; Php 3:12; 1Ti 6:12). However, he does use the single Greek word for life, *zoe* and its verb form in several significant ways, most especially to apply to the believer's life in Christ (Points 7 and 8). According to Luke, Paul even uses this Greek word to denote the natural life possessed by all animals and men (Acts 17:25).

167   Ro 8:23; Php 3:21.

This insight implies that the fullness of human salvation is future, and that fact poses a problem that should also be addressed. What does one make of Scriptures that speak of salvation as past or present?

To be sure, Scriptures indicate that being saved has reference to the past, the present, and future—all three. The author of Hebrews warns his reader not to neglect "so great a salvation."[168] Of course the gospel of salvation is multi-faceted. It targets not just one aspect of our being—our spiritual life—but addresses every dimension of human existence. Even so, here it is not important to enumerate each aspect but to search for a core idea. What is important is that first kernel of truth and understanding out of which everything else may unfold.

For the Christian, salvation refers to something in the past because he or she has already entered into union with the risen Lord, a relationship that will never end.

Salvation also pertains to life now. Jesus Christ himself is salvation, and he is present now by his Spirit within every true believer. One should not minimize this present possession of eternal life in the Spirit. Without it there is no hope of future glory. Scripture declares that in the Spirit believers have the first fruits of the future,[169] the guarantee of the coming glory.[170]

As to its fullness, salvation is still in the future. The Scripture affirms a present salvation that points to something up ahead. The book of Hebrews declares of Christ that "to those who eagerly wait for Him He will appear a second time, apart from sin, for [full] salvation."[171] For now, Christians are to put on, as a helmet,

---

168   Heb 2:3.

169   Ro 8:23.

170   Ro 8:15-17; Gal 4:6; Eph 1:14; 2Co 1:22; 5:1, 4, 5.

171   Heb 9:28.

the hope of salvation.[172] In Romans, Paul describes that salvation as the redemption of the body.[173] The salvation being described in these verses is modeled by Jesus in his resurrection. From this perspective Paul spoke of the hope of eternal life.[174] Accordingly, the goal of Paul's faith in Christ was to attain to the resurrection of the dead, that resurrection that Christ offered him through his own resurrection.[175]

How does the announcement of a future aspect of salvation relate to the proclamation of a now-present and coming kingdom of God? God is now selecting those who will be his in the coming resurrection. They comprise the advance invasion of the kingdom of God in the earth. They have been given the Spirit of God as the first fruits[176] and down payment of the resurrection life that is to come. The community of the saved—called the Church—is coextensive with his kingdom on earth because both are the domain of the Spirit of holiness released to humanity through his resurrection. According to Paul, to possess the Spirit today guarantees this salvation to come,[177] and by that Spirit one rightly claims today what is yet future. For those who believe, Jesus has abolished death and brought life and immortality to light through the gospel.[178]

In contrast to the above, many or most Christians tend to understand eternal life in a more relational and present-tense way. This is understandable and completely justified. The reason for this is two-fold: First, one major writer of the New Testament Scriptures, namely John, consistently uses the phrase *eternal life* as

---

172   1 Th 5:8.

173   Ro 8:23.

174   Tit 1:2.

175   Php 3:11–14.

176   Ro 8:23.

177   Eph 1:14.

178   2 Ti 1:10.

a present possession of believers in Christ. He even writes, "And this is eternal life, that they may know You, the only true God, and Jesus Christ whom You have sent."[179] Here is a salvation and eternal life that is relational and present now.

John is the only New Testament author to use the term *eternal life* in exactly this way. The gospel of John is usually dated to the 90s of the first century, making it one of the few second-generation documents within the canon of Scripture. If this is correct, then John's gospel falls just outside the perimeter of the intent of this book.[180] The intent was, of course, to examine the content of gospel teaching in the first generation of Christians—mostly prior to the destruction of Jerusalem in AD 70. However, even if our dating for John's writing is not quite accurate, the uniqueness of the style, message, and content in John compared to the Synoptic Gospels of Matthew, Mark, and Luke clearly reveals a further development of doctrine[181] beyond the original simplicity of the first-generation.[182]

---

179   Jn 17:3.

180   The thesis of this book does not actually depend on a late date for John's gospel, only on its internal evidence that it came after the Synoptic gospels and did not significantly inform the first Hebrew Christians. For instance, John's overall negative depiction of "the Jews" reveals a time-evolved distinction that would have been impossible for the earliest Hebrew believers. Jn 1:11; 5:10-18, 37-47; 6:41, 52; 7:10-13, 35-36; 8:22-59; 9:18-22; 10:19-24, 31-32, 39; 11:8, 53-57; 12:37-43; 18:36; 19:12, 15, 38; 20:19.

181   The Protestant doctrine of the "development of doctrine" asserts that the text of Scripture, not church tradition, provides the grounds and limits for legitimizing new doctrinal conclusions. These may grow out of historical, cultural and linguistic studies, or even the recognition of how one passage relates to another. The doctrine itself is not in the Bible but developed over time. Whatever the circular reasoning with regard to this idea, I don't deny but heartily affirm the "development of doctrine" through the end of the first century at least. That includes John's gospel, of course. Beyond the horizon of the first century, it becomes problematic to assert a scriptural precedent for justifying this doctrine, whether Catholic or Protestant.

182   This conclusion can be drawn about all John's writings. Eternal life is understood as in the present tense there too. John's epistles and Revelation were written after his gospel.

Can John's gospel be harmonized with the original first-generation understanding? Yes. John, in effect, emphasizes the Christian's secure hold on the salvation which is up ahead. Because that salvation is guaranteed by Jesus' death and resurrection and the believer's identification with him, it counts as a present possession.[183]

As already noted, Paul would emphasize the same point by highlighting the present possession of the Spirit of the Messiah as a first fruit or down payment of the eternal life to come.[184] Paul would say that "now having been set free from sin, and having become slaves of God, you have your fruit to holiness, and [in] the end [of time], everlasting life."[185] Paul, and the rest of the New Testament writers, understood salvation and eternal life like the traditional Jews of that era—as the ancient and biblical hope of future bodily resurrection.[186]

Second, this difference in the usage of words is easily explained in view of the difficulty entailed in conveying truth concerning this in-between time in history, when salvation has both come and is coming, when eternal life is assured to us now yet is future. So John's thinking was not really different, yet he used some terms with a new freedom. His usage was consistent with the idea that by the second generation the inspired doctrine was developing into its fullness within the canon.

John wanted to express the new reality of an in-between time in history, and the truth about salvation in the overlap of the two ages. Of course he knew what he was doing. This writing is not

---

183   The gospel of John is replete with statements from the mouth of Jesus that
        function proleptically. By that it is meant that something is declared as already
        true or as having already happened, when its actual occurrence is future in
        actual fact or in the chronological narrative. As for statements about eternal life,
        John's consistency from gospels to epistles should be no surprise.

184   Ro 8:23; Eph 1:14.

185   Ro 6:22.

186   Ro 8:24–25; 1Co 15:51–58; Tit 1:2.

an attempt to minimize John's contribution to the canon or to our understanding of salvation.

However, believers who only relate to John's usage can miss the core and original meaning of the biblical concept of salvation—found not just in the writings of Paul but even in the Hebraic roots of the gospel. Many Christians do not seem to understand what now should be obvious, that Jesus revealed the core meaning of these two terms—*salvation* and *eternal life*—when he rose again from the dead. To say that Jesus rose bodily from the grave as the first fruits[187] of human beings is to declare the believer's future as well, a future that embraces one's whole being, not least the bodily nature of human existence. The earliest Christians understood salvation in exactly this way.

---

187   1Co 15:20.

Twelfth Point of Truth: Saving Faith

A. In the new Christian age that has dawned, entrance into Jesus' kingdom begins with genuine faith and full acknowledgment of Jesus' identity.

B. The Bible identifies saving faith as believing from the heart that God raised Jesus from the dead (i.e., that he is the Son of God).

Point 12, the objective content of saving faith rests on the points preceding but especially on points 1 and 4 above: Christ's resurrection makes Jesus the focal point of all understanding of salvation (Point 1), in view of which he is the sovereign Lord over the Messianic kingdom prophesied to come (Point 4). That is, Jesus' resurrection and ascension fulfills the prophetic word to David that his seed would forever sit on his throne (Point 4). It follows that establishing a proper relationship to the King of the realm is crucial to participation in its benefits.

The Bible is clear about entrance requirements into the kingdom of God. A person enters that kingdom when he deliberately places himself under the rule of its king; that is, King Jesus. No one can do so, of course, until one has acknowledged Jesus in his rightful position as Lord and judge. To confess him as Lord is to do just that. Entrance into Jesus' kingdom begins with confessing Jesus to be the Lord.[188]

But this confession assumes something. The faith operating in back of any true confession is the understanding that Jesus is a living person, not deceased, not a spirit, not a ghost, and not some being in the netherworld.[189] That faith requires a resurrection, because Jesus the human had once died. When someone believes from the heart that Jesus rose from the grave as a fully functioning, operational human being, one who overcame death, then and only then is that person prepared to acknowledge his lordship as the only proper response to his triumph and victory. What King Jesus gained for himself he bestows on his subjects. This means that to believe that God raised Jesus from the dead is to put him in the highest place in the whole realm of creation, a position from which he graciously embraces all who choose to follow him.[190] Embracing them, of course, means he saves them.

That God raised Jesus from the dead should elicit amazement and awe, but the point of the matter is the message of the gospel. Jesus took on a new role at his resurrection. God raised him up from the grave to declare his identity as the Son of God, just as Paul wrote, that Jesus was "declared to be the Son of God with power according to the Spirit of holiness, by the resurrection from the dead."[191] Whenever someone confesses the preeminence, authority, or superiority of Jesus in his position at the right hand of God—whether that person confesses "Jesus is Lord" or "Jesus is the Son of God" or uses some other name or title—that person is always standing on the truth of his resurrection.[192]

---

188   Ro 10:9–10.

189   Lk 24:38–39.

190   Heb 10:12; 1Pe 3:22.

191   Ro 1:4.

192   Ro 1:4; Ac 2:24, 32; 3:15; 4:10–12; 5:30–32; 13:33–35; 17:31; Heb 5:5–6; Rev 1:18.

A simple New Testament Greek word study on *faith* and *belief* reveals something interesting. Virtually without exception, the Scriptures highlight the resurrection whenever the subject is faith in Jesus and the reason for it.[193] This fact is not coincidental. The connection of faith with resurrection can hardly be emphasized enough. The tendency is to associate the cross with faith and to neglect the resurrection almost entirely.

Addressing the Corinthians, Paul is adamant that their personal salvation hinges on the resurrection of the person of Jesus: "Now if Christ is preached that He has been raised from the dead, how do some among you say that there is no resurrection of the dead? But if there is no resurrection of the dead, then Christ is not risen. And if Christ is not risen, then our preaching is empty, and your faith is also empty."[194]

Paul views Jesus as a human being, raised from the dead. Otherwise the logic doesn't work, since the resurrection of a divine being that could never really die offers no message or hope for human beings who do die. *Paul is resting the believer's entire eternal future on his solidarity with Jesus as a bona fide human being who rose from death into eternal life.*

The eternal life Jesus attained for human beings is resurrection life—a life like the life in the body that humans have always known yet amazingly enhanced by resurrection glory. Traditionally Christians have tended to locate saving faith not in Jesus' resurrection but on the cross. Specifically believers have looked to a doctrine of atonement—a conferring of significance on Jesus' death—even beyond the simple statements of Scripture to the effect that Christ's death was for *the forgiveness of sins.* To say it more simply, evangelical Christians generally look to the

193 Mk 16:13–17; Lk 24:25–27, 40–47; Jn 2:22; 3:18, 36; 6:69; 9:35;11:25–27; 20:8, 25, 29, 31; Ac 8:37; 10:40–43; 13:28–34, 36–39; 26:22–23, 27; Ro 1:1–5; 4:24; 10:9–10; 1Co 15:1–4, 11–14; 15:17; 2Co 4:13–14; Eph 1:19–20; Col 2:12; 1Th 4:14; 1Pe 1: 3–5, 20–21; 1 Jn 1:1, 5.

194 1Co 15:12–14.

acceptance of Christ's death alone as the true door into salvation and eternal life.

To be clear about the point now being made: Christ died for the forgiveness of sins (Point 7). Moreover, God may save and receive into his kingdom persons whose objective grasp of the faith is incomplete or defective. Historically, Christians have often embraced Christ's death as atonement without much attention to the Scripture's insistence on Christ's resurrection as the saving event that it is. God knows and looks upon hearts beyond any defective understanding—and everyone is at least partially ignorant when they first approach God in response to the claims of the gospel.[195]

Given this disclaimer, look again.

In the minds of many Christians, the doctrine of the atonement rests on the idea that Christ's death on the cross functions like an Old Testament sacrifice for sins, only better. The reader encountered this thought earlier in Point 7, the common idea that believing in Jesus' sacrificial death is the key to faith. But is Jesus' death really like an Old Testament sacrifice? Well, yes—to a degree—but notice what that means. Scripturally speaking, offering up a sacrifice to God at the tabernacle or in the temple was the privilege of a covenant relationship. No individual entered into covenant with God through the sin offering or any other offering. Those sacrifices could only be offered by and for those who already belonged to the covenant people. Today, Christ's death as a sin offering functions for those who are already members of the new-covenant community. "If we confess our sins, He is faithful and just to forgive us our sins and to cleanse us from all unrighteousness."[196] John was writing to those already

---

195   I certainly don't claim one must know and receive the contents of this book in order to be saved!

196   1 Jn 1:9. Prior to John's writings Christians possessed this truth in Jesus' teaching, and in the knowledge of the new covenant and its "sure mercies of David." Lk 15:21-22; 18:13-14; Heb 8:12; Ac 13:34.

in relationship with Christ, not offering a doorway into God's family. So to the extent that Jesus' death is like an Old Testament sacrifice, it does not take on the role of granting initial acceptance with God but rather helps mediate the relationship once it has already been established.

Back to the main point. In the Bible, saving faith attaches to the conviction of Jesus' resurrection.[197] Of course, if someone believes Jesus rose in triumph from the grave, it follows that Jesus' death on the cross must be granted a unique significance of its own and was not a defeat but a victory, and it must have accomplished its purpose.

The resurrection, then, was the initial, primary key to faith.

---

197   Mk 16:13–17; Lk 24:25–27, 40–47; Jn 2:22; 3:18, 36; 6:69; 9:35;11:25–27; 20:8, 25, 29, 31; Ac 8:37; 10:40–43; 13:28–34, 36–39; 26:22–23, 27; Ro 1:1–5; 4:24; 10:9–10; 1Co 15:1–4, 11–14; 15:17; 2Co 4:13–14; Eph 1:19–20; Col 2:12; 1Th 4:14; 1Pe 1: 3–5, 20–21; 1 Jn 1:1, 5. One should note that in the fifteenth chapter of 1Co, in the one Scripture where Jesus' death for sins is made important to the content of the faith, the whole drift of Paul's thought is to emphasize the resurrection of Christ, not his death.

Thirteenth Point of Truth: New Covenant Initiation

A. Individuals are initiated into the new covenant through saving faith, repentance and water baptism.

B. Their initiation becomes complete when they receive the Holy Spirit.

Point 13 follows from points 1, 2, 4, 8, and 12. Here's how:

Throughout the New Testament Scriptures, but especially in the book of Acts, four distinct aspects of response to the gospel are mentioned as descriptive of an individual's full initiation into the new covenant. Faith, repentance, water baptism, and receiving the Holy Spirit converge to complete the set of the essential four elements.

Saving Faith

First, with reference to saving faith, Point 13 follows immediately from Point 12, which covered the content of faith. Paul's simple statement in Romans 10 says it all: "But what does it say? 'The word is near you, in your mouth and in your heart' (that is, the word of faith which we preach): that if you confess with your mouth the Lord Jesus and believe in your heart that God has raised Him from the dead, you will be saved. For with the heart one believes unto righteousness, and with the mouth confession is made unto salvation."[198]

This confession is exceedingly simple and direct, without any additions that accompanied later Church confessions or creeds. *This was the faith of the first generation of Christians.*

Repentance

True faith in Jesus is also accompanied by repentance[199]—a word that indicates a change of mind with regard to one's fundamental posture toward life and its meaning. That such a personal and inward change is an essential element of a true initiation follows from Jesus' lordship (Point 4) over the realm of the new covenant (Point 8).

Scriptural repentance involves thought, word, and deed. To repent is to think about things from God's point of view, to agree with his analysis, and to accept his verdict. The new believer may discover deeper layers of sinful depravity at a later point. But the beginning initiation, to be genuine, at the least involves the painful awareness that one is off the mark, not living life as God intended.

Repentance, to be genuine, is also specific. It involves taking honest stock of what one has actually done, and how one is living one's life. Specific sins may weigh one down; one knows they do not belong in Jesus' kingdom of righteousness. Most important, one confesses specific sins known to displease God. Those who are truly repentant choose to leave behind what is not of God.

Finally, truly repentant people follow up their conviction and verbal confession with action. In this same way, John the Baptist insisted that candidates for his baptism should first produce fruit

---

198   Ro 10:8–10.

199   Ac 2:38; 3:19; 5:31; 17:30; 20:21; 26:18, 20; Mt 3:2,8; 4:17; 21:28–32; Lk 3:3; 13:3, 5; 15:1–32; 17:3, 4; 24:47; 2Co 7:10; 2Ti 2:25.

in keeping with repentance.[200] In the case of John's followers, the action was positive. For many, however, putting things right means negative action—putting away sources of temptation and severing connections linking the person to their unrighteous past.

In a very real sense, repentance and faith may be viewed as flipsides of the same coin. John's candidates asked him, "What shall we do?"[201] This is the true response of faith—an honest desire that one's life should correspond, not conflict, with the new understanding of heart and mind. A simple confession of Jesus as Lord is both a statement of faith and an act of repentance to put away anything that interferes or conflicts with the lordship of Jesus operating in one's life.

Water Baptism

If the old covenant had its rite of initiation (circumcision), and if the new covenant has fulfilled and thus replaced the old (Point 8), it follows that there is a need for a new initiatory rite into the kingdom of God (Point 4) as an exit out of the old and into the new. Again, John the Baptist enters the picture. God provided the new initiatory rite through the advance herald of Jesus. The early idea of the meaning of baptism—for the remission of sins—came from John. He established baptism in water as a decisive action to be taken by the individual who desired God's new program for the new era of fulfillment. Baptism was picked up by Jesus' disciples from the beginning of Jesus' ministry, and, not surprisingly, Christian water baptism was sometimes said to grant the forgiveness of sins.[202] The deeper meaning of baptism had to await Jesus' trial, passion, death, and resurrection. After

---

200   Lk 3:8–14.

201   Lk 3:10, 12, 14.

202   Ac 2:38; 22:16.

Pentecost, water baptism was revealed as a ritual of union with Christ in his death and resurrection.[203]

Do thoughtful Christians sometimes struggle with the idea of the physical action of water baptism as a required part of the entrance into Jesus' heavenly kingdom? Can one treat baptism as a mere detached symbol of a spiritual event, after the fact? The first-century Christian, with his Hebrew background, would not struggle in this manner. Hebrew thought never made the mistake of separating the spiritual and physical, since the God who was Spirit created the material world.[204] Baptism is sacramental. It is a physical event with a spiritual effect. It marks the end of the old life and the beginning of the new, the end of the old human being in Adam and the resurrection of the new human being in Christ (points 9, 10, and 11). Water baptism deals decisively with the past, granting a new future in the kingdom of God.

Receive the Holy Spirit

Jesus is establishing and extending his worldwide kingdom through the Holy Spirit (Point 5). No one gets into the kingdom of God without the Holy Spirit.[205] This is so because the Holy Spirit is the very substance of the new covenant and the reality of the kingdom of God (points 4, 5, and 8).

One who hears the gospel has the opportunity to respond with faith and repentance and by being water baptized. This response is the ground upon which one receives the Holy Spirit.[206] Since the day of Pentecost, when Jesus poured out his Spirit and inaugurated

---

203 Ro 6:3–4.

204 The first clear statement of creation *ex nihilo*—the idea that the God Who is Spirit created the physical world from nothing—occurs in 2Mc 7:28 in the Apocrypha. The first-century Jew generally accepted this idea.

205 Ac 19:2,6; 2:17, 38, 39; 8:15–17; 10:44; 11:15–17; Ro 8:9, 11. In Mt 3:11 note the contrast of ritual symbol and its fulfillment.

206 Ac 2:38.

his kingdom, converts have been swept into that kingdom as God has moved upon prepared hearts. "And because you are sons, God has sent forth the Spirit of His Son into your hearts, crying out, 'Abba, Father!'"[207]

Receiving the Spirit—whatever term one uses to describe it—is the key step by which one enters into the kingdom of God.[208] Receiving the Holy Spirit constitutes actual initiation into the new covenant inaugurated by Jesus through his death and resurrection. That this must be so follows immediately from the understanding that it is through the Holy Spirit that we have the guarantee that we can receive what Christ came to give, namely, new (resurrection) life from God: "But if the Spirit of Him who raised Jesus from the dead dwells in you, He who raised Christ from the dead will also give life to your mortal bodies through His Spirit who dwells in you."[209]

Furthermore, whenever God grants the Spirit prior to water baptism, water baptism becomes the first step of obedience in the life of the believer.[210]

Conclusion

In conclusion, just as repentance and faith are flipsides of the same coin, each of the four aspects of new covenant initiation—the confession of faith, repentance, water baptism, and receiving the Spirit—should be understood in relationship to the other three, not as completely separate. A new convert rightly informed will make a confession of faith that includes repentance of sins and

---

207   Gal 4:6.

208   Ac 19:2.

209   Ro 8:11.

210   The fact that God does grant the receiving of the Spirit prior to water baptism shows us something about how these four aspects of new covenant initiation work together. First, it shows that exact order may not be so important. Second, it shows that water baptism is an initiatory rite into the new covenant community—not that without which one is necessarily lost and doomed.

will receive water baptism. God bestows the Holy Spirit on those who possess such faith. Everywhere in the New Testament—and especially in the book of Acts—this pattern of believing, responding and receiving is assumed. The early Christians evidently thought about their initiation into the faith in this integrated way. Paul linked genuine faith confession with the Holy Spirit when he wrote to the Corinthians that "no one can say that Jesus is Lord except by the Holy Spirit."[211] He wrote of water baptism,[212] of being baptized into Christ,[213] and of being baptized into Christ's body.[214] In the end he acknowledged only one baptism.[215] What is that one baptism? For Paul and the first Christians, the term *baptism* described their placement into union with Christ in his death and resurrection.[216] That placement happens by faith through the Spirit. Paul summarized when he wrote, "…having believed, you were sealed with the Holy Spirit of promise."[217]

211 1Co 12:3.

212 1Co 1:13–17.

213 Ro 6:3.

214 1Co 12:13.

215 Eph 4:5.

216 Ro 6:3–6.

217 Eph 1:13.

Fourteenth Point of Truth: The Aim of the New Covenant

A. In the new covenant, believers have been granted the status of sons of God—just like Jesus.

B. In the new covenant relationship with God, he confirms the believer's sonship status by writing his character and ways on his or her heart.

Point 14 builds on the points that have preceded it. In fact, all the preceding Dominoes have led to this one. Now comes the holy ground of God's eternal purpose, his reason for creating humans in the first place: "But when the fullness of the time had come, God sent forth His Son, born of a woman, born under the law, to redeem those who were under the law, that we might receive the adoption as sons."[218] "For you are all sons of God through faith in Christ Jesus."[219] In the new covenant, his people—both men and women—are granted the status of sons of God and become members of the God-family and recipients of God's love, just like Jesus.

But the term *sons of God* is not an honorary title with no significance. In fact, the very purpose of this new covenant is

---

218   Gal 4:4-5. See also Ro 8:14 and Eph 1:5.

219   Gal 3:26.

to grant believers the privilege and opportunity to grow into the sonship of Jesus.[220] Paul says that when God gifted his people through Jesus, he did so in order that they might "come to the unity of the faith and of the knowledge of the Son of God, to a perfect man, to the measure of the stature of the fullness of Christ."[221] "But, speaking the truth in love, [we are to] grow up in all things into Him who is the head—Christ."[222] This is the object of the new covenant.

In the Old Testament's charter passage on the new covenant, Jeremiah declared that God would forgive his people's iniquity and not remember their sin.[223] Hebrews states that Jesus became "a merciful and faithful High Priest in things pertaining to God, to make propitiation for the sins of the people."[224] Having been tempted, he is able to aid those who are tempted.[225] Jeremiah tells us this platform of mercy and forgiveness had a special purpose. God said that through the new covenant he would put his laws in the minds of his people and write them on their hearts[226]—tablets of the human heart, not stone. God's purpose from the beginning in declaring a new covenant was to fashion a people for himself. That people would be fully represented by their merciful and faithful high priest, and Jesus himself would be the example and standard to reveal the relationship between God and humanity so that they might follow in his footsteps. Every person would know God, from the least of them to the greatest.[227]

---

220 Col 1:27–28; Eph 4:13–15.

221 Eph 4:13.

222 Eph 4:15.

223 Jer 31:34.

224 Heb 2:17.

225 Heb 2:18.

226 Jer 31:33.

227 Jer 31:34.

In 2 Corinthians 3, where Paul relates his understanding of this new covenant, he begins by talking about the changed lives of his friends there, and he speaks about them with strong echoes from Jeremiah: "You are an epistle of Christ, ministered by us, written not with ink but by the Spirit of the living God, not on tablets of stone but on tablets of flesh, that is, of the heart."[228]

Change and growth into the image of Jesus is the immediate but not the final goal of the new covenant.[229] God was perfectly revealed on the earth by Jesus, who came as the first of many brothers to follow.[230] If Jesus is the Son of God, then those who are his brothers by covenant are also sons of God, being given similar rights and privileges. Born of the same parentage, they possess a corresponding heritage, identity, and destiny through the new covenant (see Point 8). That correspondence with Jesus resides in the Holy Spirit given to each one at new covenant initiation (Point 13). Through the development and manifestation of that God-given potential, God now writes his character and ways on the heart of each of Jesus' brothers.

God's people are not striving to become sons, but growing up as sons already, fully accepted in the family of God. The aim of this growth is the full stature of sonship,[231] the formation of Christ in the heart of the believer.[232]

As Paul completes his unveiling of the new covenant in 2 Corinthians 3 to 5, he moves from new covenant to new creation.

---

228   2Co 3:3; cf. Jer 31:33.

229   Paul characterized God's final goal for creation, "that God may be all in all" (1 Co 15:28). As Peter expressed it, the final goal of creation is the new heavens and a new earth "in which righteousness dwells" (2Pe 3:13). John later declared God's intent to "make all things new" (Rev 21:5).

230   Heb 2:11.

231   Eph 4:13.

232   Gal 4:19.

"Therefore, if anyone is in Christ, he is a new creation."[233] For him the old things of his old life before Christ have passed away, and all things have become new.[234] Paul is not saying that new Christians are instantly a finished product, but that everything—the entire landscape of reality itself—has become new for their sakes. Paul can celebrate the new creation that has already arrived without denying the reality of the transformation process. The context makes this clear.[235]

So in the new creation believers still need transformation—the renewal of the mind and the taming of the flesh. This involves a renovation process, one that spells out an entirely new destiny. God is transforming Christians into his image from glory to glory by his Spirit.[236]

Once the eyes of God's people open to this all-important truth—the aim of the new covenant—they are primed to discover a multitude of Scriptures that directly state or indirectly imply that God meant them to grow into Christ's very likeness.[237]

Now one can see why Jesus called for disciples, not merely people who believe. To answer the call is to *take up your cross and follow*.[238] In fact, Jesus is quite serious about this matter: "And whoever does not bear his own cross and come after Me cannot be My

---

233 2Co 5:17.

234 2Co 5:17.

235 2Co 5:20 should tell us as much. See also 2Co chapter 3. Further, Paul just finished complimenting the Corinthians on their growth in Christ based on his own ministry to them, something that took place over time. 2Co 3:3.

236 2Co 3:18.

237 Ge 1:26–27; 5:3; 9:6; Ps 17:15; Ro 1:18–23; 6:1–7; 8:3–8, 28–30; 12:2; 13:14; 1Co 11:7; 15:45–49; 2Co 3:18; 4:1–6; Eph 4:13, 17–24; Php 2:1–11; Col 1:13–22, 27; 3:5–11; 2Pe 1:5-8.

238 Mt 16:24-25; 10:38; Mk 8:34; 10:21; Lk 9:23-24; 14:27, 33.

disciple… So likewise, whoever of you does not forsake all that he has cannot be My disciple."[239]

What does this mean, in practice? The aim of the new covenant is the life of Christ replicated again and again in human beings who were designed for this very purpose. Jesus called his disciples to follow him, and Scripture commands God's people in various ways to model their lives after his.[240] No one is talking about literal imitation down to every detail, of course. No one is obligated to practice carpentry, wear seamless clothing, pursue an itinerant lifestyle, or preach from fishing vessels! However, neither is the follower of Christ supposed to drop every iota of guidance or principle and "just love" as he or she chooses to define love. Specifically, Christians should not treat the gospel accounts of Jesus' life as irrelevant, paying attention only to his teaching. Instead, one is meant to follow Jesus by understanding the overall shape and character of his life—comprising his actions, attitudes, and relationships as well as his responses, parables, and other teachings. Believers today, like Jesus' first disciples, are meant to "take up their cross and follow."

The New Testament Scriptures in their entirety unfold truths that impact hearts and lives at every level of understanding and practice.[241] Then too there are the Old Testament Scriptures, written for New Testament believers even if not to them. Paul told Timothy that the Hebrew Scripture was "given by inspiration of God, and is profitable for doctrine, for reproof, for correction, for instruction in righteousness."[242] He said they were "able to

239   Lk 14:27, 33.

240   Eph 5:3; Php 2:5; 1Pe 2:2ff.

241   The observation that the first Christians did not enjoy what others do today—namely, a completed canon of Scripture—in no way compromises the aim of the new covenant. The first Christians had something later believers would not—the advantage of the preaching and teaching of the original apostles and their disciples. Even more to the point, they had the same Holy Spirit.

242   2Ti 3:16.

make you wise for salvation through faith which is in Christ Jesus."[243] Paul affirmed their new covenant role in maturing the saint of God, "that the man of God may be complete, thoroughly equipped for every good work."[244]

There is a caution, however. Paul says "the letter kills, but the Spirit gives life."[245] Transformation comes from the work of the Holy Spirit in the heart, not a slavish mentality toward the letter of the Scriptures themselves. The Spirit of God must illumine the Scriptures just as he must illumine each Christian's heart and life. God's people are not to be looking to Scripture by itself as their ticket to transformation, but they are to be guided by the Holy Spirit—who illuminates Scripture—to live in the reality of Jesus living his life through theirs. In the dynamic of the new covenant this happens only as believers engage the whole process of transformation "with unveiled face, beholding as in a mirror the glory of the Lord."[246] In this way they "are being transformed into the same image from glory to glory, just as by the Spirit of the Lord."[247]

However one may use the Scriptures, one fact remains supreme. *The power of the new covenant for transformation comes from the Spirit of God.* The Spirit of God is the very essence of what it means to be "in the kingdom" (Point 5). Receiving the Holy Spirit marks the complete initiation into the new covenant inaugurated by Jesus through his death and resurrection (Point 13). The aim of the new covenant is that believers might follow Christ and grow up in him in all things through the Holy Spirit's

---

243 2Ti. 3:15.

244 2Ti 3:17.

245 2Co 3:6.

246 2 Co. 3:18.

247 2Co 3:18.

leadership. "For as many as are led by the Spirit of God, these are sons of God."[248]

In this way, every follower of Christ will—in his or her own way— move along God's path, allowing the Spirit of God to do what he always does as the believer beholds Jesus. True saints follow hard after him, and they are transformed into his image. The first Christians, enlightened by the original gospel, understood this transformation as the aim of the new covenant.

---

248 Ro 8:14.

Fifteenth Point of Truth: Accountability to God

A. Every human being will stand before King Jesus to give an account of his or her life.

B. Justification by faith proclaims in advance our favorable outcome at the judgment seat of Christ.

Now the issue of accountability to God for the aim and goal of one's personal history on Earth must be examined. In Point 10 it was stated that the final verdict on the Christian's future was ahead and would forever seal his or her destiny. Point 11 explored the nature of the salvation to be granted or denied. Points 12 and 13 covered what it means to enter into salvation now. Point 14 considered God's aim and purpose in the new covenant. In this whole scheme God holds his people accountable for what he wants. So Point 15 rests squarely on all the preceding dominoes.

The Jews had taught for centuries before Christ that at the end of time, God's people—indeed, all people—would come before God to be judged for their deeds on Earth. God was an impartial judge, and he would punish or reward both Jews and Gentiles according to what they deserved.[249] No Jew was given a free pass to eternal bliss based on the claim to membership among the chosen people.

---

249 See all of Ro 2, especially Ro 2:5–11.

Given that the gospel's origin was Jewish, that Jesus and Paul were Jews, and that the first Christians were Jews, it simply cannot be that the original apostolic teaching ignored this whole Jewish matter of eternal judgment. And, of course, it did not.[250] The Bible is clear that Jesus is God's judge at the end of the age.[251] God will judge all humans through Jesus Christ. As his servants, Christians too will each give a personal accounting of their lives directly to him. The difference between the Jewish teaching and the Christian is *not* that there is no judgment for the Christian. Rather, it is that the Christian will indeed be judged by One who is his Lord, but the One who is also committed to be his Savior, saving him from ultimate condemnation but not necessarily from loving discipline.

This understanding leads to an astounding insight. The concept that no Christian could ever be punished or even reprimanded at the judgment seat of Christ is popular teaching but needs a careful rethinking. Consider what Jesus told his disciples.

> "Who then is that faithful and wise steward, whom his master will make ruler over his household, to give them their portion of food in due season? Blessed is that servant whom his master will find so doing when he comes. Truly, I say to you that he will make him ruler over all that he has. But if that servant says in his heart, 'My master is delaying his coming,' and begins to beat the male and female servants, and to eat and drink and be drunk, the master of that servant will come on a day when he is not looking for him, and at an hour when he is not aware, and will cut him in two and appoint him his portion with the unbelievers. And that servant who knew his master's will, and did not prepare himself or do

250 See, for example, Heb 6:2.

251 Ac 18:31; Jn 5:22.

according to his will, shall be beaten with many stripes. But he who did not know, yet committed things deserving of stripes, shall be beaten with few. For everyone to whom much is given, from him much will be required; and to whom much has been committed, of him they will ask the more."[252]

Paul also writes, "For we must all appear before the judgment seat of Christ, that each one may receive the things done in the body, according to what he has done, whether good or bad."[253] Then Paul writes, "Knowing, therefore, the terror of the Lord, we persuade men."[254] Clearly, the Spirit of God who inspired Paul intended that the *terror* of the judgment seat of Christ would motivate believers.

Again, the Jews of Jesus' day understood that there was to be a day in which God would judge every human being and would "render to each one according to his deeds': eternal life to those who by patient continuance in doing good seek for glory, honor, and immortality; but to those who are self-seeking and do not obey the truth, but obey unrighteousness—indignation and wrath, tribulation and anguish, on every soul of man who does evil."[255] When Paul wrote these words in Romans, he was not being uniquely Christian but merely setting forth the standard Jewish perspective.

How did Christians come to omit this important truth? It is generally understood that the term *bema*—the Greek word for "judgment-seat"—is used in the New Testament to indicate a platform where contestants in a contest receive their laurels. Quite the contrary, the Greek word bema—used twelve times in the

---

252   Lk 12:42–48.

253   2Co 5:10.

254   2Co 5:11.

255   Ro 2:6–10.

New Testament[256]—never once refers to a place where trophies are awarded. Instead, bema refers consistently to an elevated seat where a person accused of a crime is brought for judgment.

Every human being, including every Christian, will pass before Jesus Christ and be judged according to his or her works.[257] This is the consistent and sole testimony of Scripture concerning the judgment. The Scripture never says anyone will be judged by their faith—only their works. Furthermore, even the judgment at the white throne in the book of Revelation is not a separate judgment but part of the judgment seat of Christ. How can someone know this? Because the Father declares he has already given all authority and power of judgment to Jesus Christ.[258]

For anyone who comes to God through Christ, divine grace forgives their sins, grants them new status as sons of God, and gives them the Holy Spirit so they can approach God and receive the power and wisdom from heaven to enable them to live righteously.[259]

A problem arises, though, in understanding how one can rejoice in one's present standing with God, as someone justified by faith apart from works of the law, and yet be judged in a future judgment which is all about works.

Beginning with the Jewish understanding of the judgment of God, Paul works through this issue in the book of Romans. When a person first believes in "[the God] who raised Jesus our Lord from the dead,"[260] that person is justified by faith—completely

---

256 Mt 27:19; Jn 19:13; Ac 7:5; 12:21; 18:12, 16, 17; 25:6, 10, 17; Ro 14:10; 2Co 5:10.

257 Mt 16:27; Rev 2:23; 20:12–13; 22:12; Ps 62:12; Ro 2:6; 2Co 5:10; 11:15; Jer 17:10; 32:19; Ecc 12:14; Pr 24:12, 29; 2Ti 4:14.

258 Jn 5:22; Ac 10:42.

259 Ro 8:2, 5, 9, 11, 13–14.

260 Ro 4:24.

apart from the deeds of the Torah (i.e., the old covenant).[261] But then "having been set free from sin, and having become slaves of God, you have your fruit to holiness, and the end, everlasting life."[262] So how does one go from becoming a Christian to having "fruit to holiness"? To be a Christian is to have the Holy Spirit, and the Holy Spirit supplies what is needful and eliminates the inconsistency between present standing and future judgment.

The Spirit of Christ in every believer—if yielded to—brings forth the testimony of a life that gains God's approval at the judgment: "Therefore, brethren, we are debtors—not to the flesh, to live according to the flesh. For if you live according to the flesh you will die; but if by the Spirit you put to death the deeds of the body, you will live. For as many as are led by the Spirit of God, these are sons of God."[263]

According to Paul, the verdict on a Christian at the final judgment is not just automatic. Paul is writing to Christians when he declares, "If you live according to the flesh you will die." However, the emphasis is actually positive, not merely a warning. "[Since] by the Spirit you [do] put to death the deeds of the body, you [can know in advance that you] will live."[264] The declaration that Christians are now justified by faith anticipates the final verdict to be given at Christ's judgment seat. The warrant for this verdict given in advance is the fact that believers have already received the Spirit of Christ—the Spirit of the One who overcame sin and death. Jesus triumphed, gained for himself the favorable verdict, and offers

---

261 In Ro 3:28–29 Paul writes that "one is justified by faith apart from works of the law." But the sentence does not end there. He goes on saying "or is God the God of the Jews only?" Paul is attacking the attitude that uses the law to distinguish Jew from Gentile and set up Old Testament Israel as God's special chosen people, the doorway into all God's purposes.

262 Ro 6:22.

263 Ro. 8:12–14.

264 Ro 8:13. Basically Paul is referring, of course, to the great hope of future eternal life, the kind described by Jesus in his resurrection body. This insight, however, does not preclude a present-tense application.

to everyone his overcoming spirit through the Holy Spirit in the new covenant. In everyone who receives his life the Spirit works the attitudes, motives, and character of Christ. Out of that life in God one does those deeds that demonstrate one's true identity[265] and will result in that same favorable verdict. Hence Christians have a sure hope for the future, that in the final evaluation they will be declared righteous just as they have already been declared righteous in anticipation of their future destiny.

This is exactly what Paul means when he says, "For we through the Spirit eagerly wait for the hope of righteousness by faith."[266] In light of the Holy Spirit's work within and through believers, that righteousness is the final verdict on the believer's character.

This does not mean God is demanding perfection. Rather, it indicates that at the judgment God will find what he is looking for: "gold, silver, precious stones,"[267] the evidence of a life that "will receive a reward."[268]

---

265   Eph 2:10.

266   Gal 5:5.

267   1Co 3:12.

268   1Co 3:14.

Sixteenth Point of Truth: Personal Destiny

A. The full salvation Jesus offers is defined by his resurrection and is future—a bodily, immortal, glorified life.

B. To be outside Jesus' kingdom is to be lost and without hope of eternal life.

If the reader will carefully gather the full understanding that is offered by the preceding dominoes, the sixteenth point of truth should become apparent.

In the end, salvation is both granted and defined by the resurrection of Jesus. Christians will be raised in resurrection life into the world to come, a world that must correspond to the present physical world enough that one's life in resurrection will be a life in the body—albeit, a body enhanced in powers and expression to be like the glorified body of our Lord Jesus.[269] This is the original Christian hope.

Because the first Christians knew Jesus' resurrection had meaning not only for him but for their destiny as well, many naturally tended to assume Christ would return within their lifetime. In particular, Paul's early evangelistic efforts in Thessalonica had given rise to an assembly of believers with this expectation. When

---

269 Php 3:21.

some died but Jesus had not returned, Paul's converts began to despair for their fate, assuming one must be alive to benefit from Christ's second coming. In response, Paul exhorts them not to grieve as pagans do "who have no hope [for the dead]."[270] "For if we believe that Jesus died and rose again, even so God will bring with Him those who sleep in Jesus."[271] Paul's assurance that deceased believers will be raised with Christ at his coming informs Christians today as well. For throughout his letters, Paul uses the word *hope* not only to address with comfort questions about mortality but to supply the content of the answer.[272]

In the New Testament, therefore, the word *hope* takes on a new, enhanced significance. For the Christian, *hope* is assured; it is directed to the future, and its content is the resurrection. "Not only that, but we also who have the firstfruits of the Spirit, even we ourselves groan within ourselves, eagerly waiting for the adoption, the redemption of our body. For we were saved in this hope."[273]

God has "given us everlasting consolation and good hope by grace."[274] Future resurrection life—the Christian hope—is the exclusive domain of the risen Messiah, whose plan is to liberate the entire creation through his sons.[275] For now, however, the kingdom of God is comprised of those who have been initiated into this hope.

If someone truly believes the Christian gospel, there is no other hope.[276] To reject this good news is to turn down the only hope

---

270 1 Th 4:13.

271 1 Th 4:14.

272 Ro 8:20, 23–24; 5:2; 12:12; 15:4, 13; 1Co 13:13; Gal 5:5; Eph 2:12; Col. 1:27; 1Th 5:8; 2Th 2:16; Tit 2:11–13; Heb 6:18–19; 1Pe 1:3, 21.

273 Ro 8:23–24.

274 2 Th 2:16.

275 Ro 8:19–22.

276 1 Th 4:13–14. This is exactly what Paul is saying, especially in light of 2 Th 1:7–10.

that God has given humanity, setting aside the only one who offers this hope, and the only one capable of granting its realization. God raised Jesus from the grave to give human beings the hope of eternal life.[277] To be outside that kingdom is to be without hope. Paul preached this in his travels, and Matthew and other first-generation Christians agreed.[278]

Whatever one may think to say about people in their various paths of life and consequent destinies, one's place of inheritance in Christ's kingdom is to be secured now, in this life. "Behold, now is the accepted time; behold, now is the day of salvation."[279] Humanity has now arrived at that fullness of time (Point 10) when people are making their final decision to accept or reject the path to salvation that God has now fully laid out in Christ.[280]

Bible-believing Christians have chosen to be among those who are counted as sheep—not goats. They have chosen to be found among those who inherit the kingdom, the eternal kingdom received at the final approval given by the Son of Man.

Finally, it needs to be said that the first Christians never rested on the knowledge of their initiation into the faith (Point 13)—as in, "I know I'm saved because I had a conversion experience." To them, the faith was very much the running of a race[281]—a race one needed to win. The mark or goal was the finish line, not the starting line.

---

277 Tit 1:2.

278 Mt 25:31–34, 41, 46.

279 2Co 6:2.

280 As much as possible, I avoid stretching the reader with dogmatic statements about issues beyond the scope of this book. The destiny of the unbeliever is another such issue—not to mention those who do not, or did not, believe in Christ because they never heard the truth.

281 1Co 9:24-27; Gal 5:7; Php 2:16; 3:10-14; 2Th 4:7.

If we take Paul as an example, one will not win the crown until one has reached the end of life's journey.[282] Until then, one needs to be stripped of every hindrance. In Philippians, he writes, "Yet indeed I also count all things loss for the excellence of the knowledge of Christ Jesus my Lord, for whom I have suffered the loss of all things, and count them as rubbish, that I may gain [win] Christ."[283]

When he wrote this, Paul already had an unparalleled record of ministry behind him. What more could he do to achieve his personal goals? If successful ministry was the target, then Paul had already hit the bull's-eye. What, then, is the meaning of his longing, "that I may win Christ"? "[I long to] know Him and the power of His resurrection, and the fellowship of his sufferings, being conformed to his death, if, by any means, I may attain to the resurrection [out] from the dead."[284]

Here, Paul discloses his deepest inner cry—to know Christ, the power of his resurrection, and the fellowship of his sufferings. He wants to be made like Jesus in his death. Here is Paul's objective—to attain that resurrection that lifts one out of the realm of the dead—just like Jesus, ahead of all the rest.[285] This is what he meant by "winning Christ."

Paul doesn't tell the Philippians here that "Jesus paid the price" or that "Jesus did it all for us." He doesn't focus on his initial conversion to Christ. Instead, he looks forward, commending to them the aim of the new covenant (Point 14), the image of Christ replicated in each of his followers. After this, Paul admits he will do anything to assure the desired outcome. His perspective may be hard to understand today. Modern Christians may excuse their own failings in their Christian walk, resting in the comforting

282 2Ti 4:6–8.

283 Php 3:8.

284 Php 3:10–11.

285 Ac 26:23.

thought that God must also excuse them, since no one is perfect. To some, excusing may seem the only possible alternative to despair.[286]

But Paul did not excuse his own failings. He did not despair, either. Instead, he lived in the hope of the gospel, making it his glorious pursuit. Thinking in terms of ongoing discipleship, one should be able to grasp Paul's drift.[287] "Not that I have already attained, or am already perfected; but I press on, that I may lay hold of that for which Christ Jesus has also laid hold of me. Brethren, I do not count myself to have apprehended; but one thing I do, forgetting those things which are behind and reaching forward to those things which are ahead, I press toward the goal for the prize of the upward call of God in Christ Jesus."[288]

Then, in 1 Corinthians, Paul again tells his converts that the Christian life is like running a race, with the possibility of either winning or not: "Do you not know that those who run in a race all run, but one receives the prize? Run in such a way that you may obtain it. And everyone who competes for the prize is temperate in all things. Now they do it to obtain a perishable crown, but we for an imperishable crown. Therefore I run thus: not with uncertainty. Thus I fight [box]: not as one who beats the air. But I discipline my

---

286   The province of Paul's thinking is ongoing discipleship, not initial salvation. So, although someone could react here, saying, "But I thought God does excuse our sins at the cross!" there is no ground to this objection. Furthermore, excusing means to find us not guilty in the first place, something the gospel message does not do.

287   Heb 4:9–11. Even if Paul did not write Hebrews, he would certainly agree with the one who did, and he would assure us that the true rest of faith and the passionate pursuit to win Christ harmonize completely.

288   Php 3:12–14.

body and bring it into subjection,[289] lest, when I have preached to others, I myself should become disqualified."[290]

Paul said he buffeted his body like a boxer, handled it roughly, and disciplined it by hardships. He says, "Brethren, join in following my example, and note those who so walk, as you have us for a pattern [example]."[291] Paul's approach is not supposed to be unique to him as an apostle. Every true disciple should have the same attitude. God provided Paul and other early Christians as inspiring examples.

Christians have been saved—in the sense of receiving a promise and a down payment (Point 13)—they are being saved—in the sense that they are working out the character that answers the aim and purpose (Point 14)—and they will be saved—in the sense of their final and full salvation (Points 10 and 11). Each one will render an account of his or her life at the judgment seat of Christ (Point 15). Jesus, who is both the Christian's advocate and judge, will render the final verdict on each one at that time. That verdict will be given in accordance with the manner and extent to which the individual has cooperated with God as they have worked out Christ's death and resurrection in their lives.

If we are genuine Christians, then, like Paul, we have already heard in our spirits something of the call of the original gospel. We already know something of the message of the new covenant—this message of the availability of the eternal life of God through the One who died and rose again. We have the opportunity to respond, and we know how to respond. Our lives last but a brief moment, something we cannot afford to waste.

---

289   The literal Greek is informative. "I beat my body black and blue—smiting myself so as to cause bruises and livid spots—and bring it into slavery, lest after preaching to others I myself should be rejected."

290   1Co 9:24–27.

291   Php 3:17.

If, like the first-generation Christians, we have heard the good news, we owe it to ourselves to fully enter the race, to aim for "the prize of the upward call of God in Christ Jesus."[292]

292   Php 3:14.

The Complete Set of Domino Truths

1. Jesus of Nazareth, crucified on a cross, has been raised bodily from the dead into glorified, everlasting life.

2. It was God—the God of the Jews—who raised Jesus from the dead, thus declaring Jesus to be God's special agent to accomplish his will and purpose.

3. Jesus is the Anointed One, the Jewish Messiah, the Christ predicted by the Torah and all the prophets.

4. The Jews—in effect—crucified their own Messiah!

5. A crucified Messiah who rose again demands a reinterpretation of Jewish messianic expectations.

6. The time of the fulfillment of God's end-time promises to Israel in Torah and the prophets has now arrived.

7. Jesus' resurrection and ascension fulfills the prophetic word to David that his descendant would sit on his throne forever.

8. Jesus is Lord over a kingdom, one that functions from heaven but has invaded the earth.

9. Jesus is the true descendant of Abraham who has received the promised blessing for the nations.

10. Jesus extends his kingdom everywhere by pouring out his Spirit.

11. As far as God's purposes are concerned, the time of the separation of the Jews and Gentiles is over.

12. Jesus' death has nullified the curse of the law and set the law aside as the way to God.

13. Because of the resurrection, the cross of Jesus was not a defeat but a victory.

14. The cross was the supreme occasion of God's mercy.

15. Jesus died and rose again to establish the new covenant.

16. The new covenant is the charter of the kingdom of God, fulfilling and thus superseding all previous covenants God made with Israel.

17. The new covenant reaches all the way back to Adam in its scope.

18. Jesus is Adam's true replacement; he succeeds where Adam failed, and he cancels the curse of death.

19. The risen Messiah created a new future for Israel, those who belong to Jesus, the human race, and the entire universe.

20. People today are living in a new in-between time in history, when Messiah reigns in the midst of his enemies until his return.

21. The resurrection of Jesus is the foundation and real explanation of the salvation he offers.

22. The redemption of the body is the bedrock meaning of eternal life.

23. In the new Christian age that has dawned, entrance into Jesus' kingdom begins with genuine heart faith and full acknowledgment of Jesus' identity.

24. The Bible identifies saving faith as believing from the heart that God raised Jesus from the dead (i.e., that he is the Son of God).

25. Individuals are initiated into the new covenant through saving faith, repentance and water baptism.

26. Their initiation becomes complete when they receive the Holy Spirit.

27. In the new covenant believers have been granted the status of sons of God—just like Jesus.

28. In the new covenant relationship with God, he confirms the believer's sonship status by writing his character and ways on his or her heart.

29. Every human being will stand before King Jesus to give an account of his or her life.

30. Justification by faith proclaims in advance our favorable outcome at the judgment seat of Christ.

31. The full salvation Jesus offers is defined by his resurrection and is future—a bodily, immortal, glorified life.

32. To be outside Jesus' kingdom is to be lost and without hope of eternal life.

Conclusion

When Paul was being tried at Caesarea, in an ordeal initiated by the highly incensed Jews who had come down from Jerusalem, the question rose as to the actual nature of the charges against him. What was the Jewish complaint all about, anyway? So Paul was permitted to speak in his own defense. Relating at first the story of his life growing up and then as a Pharisee, he proceeded to tell of his encounter with the risen Christ on the Damascus Road. In the process, he relayed personal convictions that help to conclude this investigation of the first-generation gospel: "And now I stand and am judged for the hope of the promise made by God to our fathers. To this promise our twelve tribes, earnestly serving God night and day, hope to attain. For this hope's sake, King Agrippa, I am accused by the Jews. Why should it be thought incredible by you that God raises the dead?"[293]

First, to Paul, true Judaism did not conflict with the message he proclaimed. There was no discontinuity. He was attempting, according to his testimony, not to establish a new religion but to proclaim something predicted by Moses and the prophets: "Therefore, having obtained help from God, to this day I stand, witnessing both to small and great, saying no other things than those which the prophets and Moses said would come—that the Christ would suffer, that He would be the first to rise from the dead, and would proclaim light to the Jewish people and to the Gentiles."[294]

---

293   Ac 26:6–8.

294   Ac 26:22–23.

Second, Paul defends himself in the two summary statements above, and in both cases he makes one other thing extremely clear. Everything he has to say is about resurrection—resurrection as the fulfillment of the hope of the ancient Hebrew fathers and the meaning of the sacred Hebrew Scriptures.

Paul's example illustrates the two main points of the thesis in this book:

First, although Jesus' death and resurrection together constitute the foundation of the original faith, the resurrection of Jesus is clearly the foundational key into the gospel, not the cross. There is simply no way to unpack the meaning of the good news of the gospel and salvation without the right starting point. Every point of this thesis, every domino in this string of dominoes, every conclusion depends upon this insight.

Second, Jude exhorts his reader to contend earnestly for the faith that was once for all delivered to the saints. However, that faith was first given primarily to Jews, not Gentiles. This means that one of the cardinal litmus tests for discerning the basics of that faith is a "Jewish compatibility test." Would a first-century Jew be able to receive the good news even though it challenged some of his commonly accepted notions of the precise relationship of Israel with Messiah? The original gospel message had to have been congruent to him on a number of fronts. Certainly it did not require him to immediately renounce his deeply held Jewish convictions in favor of another religion! The first-century Christian message to the Jew first was not about changing religions but about the fulfillment of his own! For him, Jesus came not to destroy the law but to fulfill it.[295] If Christians cannot structure their presentation of the gospel so that it reflects the first-century foundation, they may be ignorant of the faith at it was actually "once for all delivered." They may not really even understand the actual gospel.

---

295   Mt 5:17.

Christians should, of course, recognize valid doctrinal developments of succeeding centuries. However, all later valid doctrinal developments had to have had a viable platform from which they sprang originally, and *basic Christian understanding should not start somewhere other than at the beginning.* This book is not about all that should be believed as a Christian. It is about recognizing origins and hidden foundations. It is about the *kerygma,* the core of true gospel teaching. It's about beginning at the source of the faith—the resurrection of Christ as a saving event—and developing everything else from it.

Postscript

Readers should not be surprised to discover that the final and complete result of this effort to reconstruct the first-generation gospel looks remarkably compatible with the ancient Apostle's Creed—both in what each does and does not say. Although as far as scholars know the creed itself was not written in the first generation, its very name indicates that those who composed it did so in the conviction that they were anchoring the people of God on a first-generation foundation. The presence of the creed among the earliest known Christian documents corroborates the thesis of this book.

On a last note, however, perhaps what has been most surprising on this journey is just how many of the most common Christian doctrines I have omitted from discussion for the sake of the topic at hand. My "set of dominoes" is intended to capture only the very earliest version of the Christian message. If one is to clearly grasp the earliest Christian thinking, one must also understand something of the order in which doctrines developed.

For instance, first-generation Christians did not have to settle the issue of whether Jesus was lower than or equal to the Father. Their gospel at that time left open possibilities. They proclaimed their good news without the example or the influence of the principal second-generation document that would serve to catapult the believing community on a whole new trajectory—the gospel of John. Let no one minimize the principal truth God revealed through John's gospel. Jesus is indeed "the Word [who] became flesh"[296]—with all this implies both about his humanity and his divinity. The full canon of gospel truth is incomplete without John's writing, of course. But the thesis of this book is predicated upon the conviction that the earliest gospel understanding was a self-contained package that should be recognized even without the second-generation additions. The good news of Jesus Christ was given first to the Jew and then to the Greek.[297] First came the Hebraic-based perspective; that is, the first-generation perspective. This foundational teaching of the early apostles should structure thinking about the faith—not to stop there but to build on it. Reader, are you willing to let the first things be first? If anyone wants to build a solid structure that can handle future stresses, there is no substitute for a proper foundation.

Scripture mandates this structuring. Jude exhorts his readers to "contend earnestly for the faith which was once for all delivered to the saints."[298] If Christians believe Jude was writing Holy Scripture, they become responsible to contend for the same thing. That mandate explains the reason for this book.

---

296 Jn 1:14.

297 Ro 1:16.

298 Jude 3. Scholars date the epistle of Jude from 66 to 80 AD, most likely before 70 AD. Jude's concern for the "faith once delivered" must be considered a cry to preserve the very gospel I have attempted to unpack.

About the Author

James (Jim) Leuschen has formally been in the ministry since 1980, when he established New Covenant Fellowship, an independent non-denominational church located in Spokane, Washington. Prior to that time he had attended an independent evangelical church which emphasized the raising up of young adults into the Christian ministry. There he was shaped for life and trained for ministry. He was ordained in 1970.

Jim has made a lifelong study of the Scriptures, early church history, early church writings, and theology. Known as a profound teacher of the Word, he has ministered in other churches and conferences and also edits others' writings. This current volume was preceded by his book, *Good News for Mortal Man: The Resurrection Gospel of the Early Church* as well as a smaller condensed version of the same material. He also wrote *How to Achieve Church Unity*.

Jim was born in Seattle, Washington, grew up in the Northwest and attended Whitworth College in Spokane, Washington. He majored in mathematics, and received the President's Cup for graduating first in his class in 1969. After obtaining a master's degree in mathematics, he taught math and physics at a college preparatory high school but soon switched careers and went into full-time Christian ministry. Jim's inductive and systematic approach to understanding Scripture has been shaped both by his study over forty years and also by his own academic background and education.

Jim resides in Spokane with his wife, Marcia, who pastors the church with him. He is an avid reader in theology, apologetics, philosophy, history and science and enjoys hanging out with two young boys to whom he is *Papa*.

Jim can be contacted through his website www.advancingtruth. org or by e-mail at jameseleuschen@gmail.com.